Soul Winner's Fire

Soul Winner's Fire

John R. Rice

Printed in the United States of America

Table of Contents

Preface

As a fifteen year old boy, I had my first taste of the joy of soul winning. I persuaded a friend to confess himself a sinner and look to Christ for salvation. Since that day it has been the longing of my soul to bring people to trust in Christ as their personal Saviour.

These chapters appeared at various times in the SWORD OF THE LORD. Each one was planned for a particular time and occasion; now they have been selected for this book as centering around soul winning and revival. I trust the dear Lord will use them to warm and make tender the hearts of God's people in a deep concern for a lost world.

Three principal thoughts seem especially urgent to me: first, that every Christian ought to win souls; second, that we ought to have a holy passion, a tearful and compelling earnestness, an apostolic fervor of soul; and third, that we must have a divine enablement of the Holy Spirit.

By saving souls we do not mean getting people to join the church, or to be merely reformed, or to go through certain religious rites. We believe that the whole world lies in sin. People are all undone, lost, ruined sinners who cannot save themselves. Not an outward change in the life, but an inward change in the heart, a new birth by which one becomes a born-again child of God, with all sins forgiven—that is what every man and woman, and every child who has reached the age of accountability needs. Christ died on the cross to put away the sin of the whole world. Those who trust in Him, in penitent faith accepting Him as their Saviour, depending on Him for forgiveness of their sins and everlasting life and a home in Heaven, are saved and become the children of God.

So to be a soul winner means to cause people to realize their need of Christ as personal Saviour and to lead them to commit themselves wholly to Him, with heart faith. A sinner who does so trust Christ is a forgiven child of God, and one who leads the sinner to make this heart decision is a soul winner.

Oh, the blessed rewards God has for the soul winner!

Nothing is clearer in the Bible than this: every Christian can and ought to win souls. Andrew won Peter. Philip won Nathaniel. Jesus won the woman at the well of Sychar in Samaria, and she in turn won so many of her townspeople. Every Christian may have the marvelous privilege of winning souls.

Dear reader, if God stirs your heart, will you not start out at once to win souls to Christ?

It is the humble prayer of the author that God may use these simple messages to start soul-winning fires and to cause many Christians to introduce lost sinners to the Saviour. Grant it, O God!

JOHN R. RICE

"He That Winneth Souls Is Wise"

"The fruit of the righteous is a tree of life; and he that winneth souls is wise."—Prov. 11:30.

It is the wise person who takes the long look. How foolish to think only of today with its passing pleasure or profit! Esau is a classic example of the man who thought only of the pleasures of today. He sold his birthright for a mess of pottage. Afterwards he found no place of repentance, though he sought it carefully with tears. He threw away his opportunity to be the head of a great race, the ancestor of Jesus Christ, for a bowl of chili. On that account, the Bible calls Esau that "profane person." Whatever faults Jacob had, he did take the long look.

Jacob was given spiritual wisdom, and sacrificed, suffered and sweated to receive the promised blessing in the uncounted years ahead. The best estimate of these two—the folly of Esau and the wisdom of Jacob—is expressed in the words of the Lord: "Jacob have I loved, but Esau have I hated."

Abraham was wise; Lot was foolish. Abraham counted himself a sojourner and lived in tents all his days, as did Isaac and Jacob, heirs with him of the same promise. Hebrews 11:13–16 tells us:

> "These all died in faith, not having received the promises, but having seen them afar off, and were persuaded of them, and embraced them, and confessed that they were strangers and pilgrims on the earth. For they that say such things declare plainly that they seek a country. And truly, if they had been mindful of that country from whence they came out, they might have had opportunity to have returned. But now they desire a better country, that is, an heavenly: wherefore God is not ashamed to be called their God: for he hath prepared for them a city."

That heavenly wisdom of Abraham, who by faith took the long look, will never be fully justified until the New Jerusalem comes down from God out of Heaven, and Abraham dwells in eternal happiness in the land of Palestine, made new like the Garden of Eden, in the presence of Christ and the Father with all the redeemed. On the other hand, Lot, who was enamored by the riches of this world, moved into Sodom and there saw the ruin of his home, the death of his wife, and later was guilty of drunken shame with his own daughters. Lot sought the things of today, but Abraham looked to the morrow. Lot chose the things that are seen, which are temporal, while Abraham chose the things that are unseen, which are eternal (II Cor. 4:18).

Every day I see those who take the short look and live

only for today. Their thoughts and efforts are centered on food, clothing, jobs, business, pleasure, which are enjoyed for a moment or a day or a year, and then vanish away.

The Wisdom of the Soul Winner in the Light of the Worth of a Soul

"He that winneth souls is wise." We may put it down, on the authority of Holy Writ, that the best wisdom of this world is not shown by the banker nor by the statesman nor by the educator nor by the millionaire businessman, but by the humble soul winner. All other labor is insignificant beside the supreme labor of winning souls. All other efforts are as good as wasted when the results they bring are considered beside the eternal and glorious results of soul winning.

The Saviour Himself indicated that one soul is worth more than all the world: "For what shall it profit a man, if he shall gain the whole world, and lose his own soul? Or what shall a man give in exchange for his soul?" (Mark 8:36, 37).

Certain considerations help us to see the value of a soul, and I want to suggest them for your prayerful meditation. Our fathers were accustomed to pray, "Lord, roll on us the weight of immortal souls." Again and again I have heard that heartfelt petition as men besought God to give them a Heaven-born concern for the salvation of sinners. That prayer I heard often in my childhood, and I make it my own again today.

Soul winning is such a delicate art, it requires such a heavenly wisdom, it weighs so little in the minds of worldly men, that we are not likely to win souls unless we consider some appalling and glorious facts that bear on the subject. Suppose we think about the fact of Hell, the ruin and misery of this world, the death of Christ, and the glories of Heaven, as they bear on soul winning.

The Fact of Hell

I suppose the most horrible, concrete fact in all the world is that of Hell. The doctrine of Hell has a most prominent place in the Bible. Even Jesus Himself, who spake as never man spake, the tender and lowly One, the forgiving, the healing, the comforting Jesus, referred again and again to the place called Hell. The most startling things ever said in the Bible about it came from His lips.

It was Jesus who said that the worm does not die and the fire is not quenched in Hell.

It was Jesus who said that men should be cast both soul and body into Hell.

It was Jesus who opened for us the lid of Hell and let us hear the cries of the doomed rich man who lifted up his eyes in torment and begged for one drop of water to cool his tongue, as he was tormented in flames!

If any man has a heart, a soul, he ought to be profoundly moved at the thought of one human being going to that place!

Let us be honest about it; the Bible does teach that Hell is a place. It teaches that men are conscious there, that men remember there, that they cry out, beg for water, long to warn their loved ones, "lest they also come into this place of torment." The Bible does teach that the smoke of their torment in Hell ascends up forever and ever, and that they have no rest day or night. It does teach that all the impenitent who die without Christ wake up in the terrible world of eternal punishment. The Scripture makes clear that at the resurrection of the unjust, the unsaved dead will come out of Hell only long enough to get physical bodies and then be sentenced forever to the unending doom of the lake of fire (Rev. 20)!

If they believe the Bible, honest people will not quibble about a literal Hell. If Hell is not a fact, then the inspiration of the Bible is not a fact. If Hell is not a fact, then the deity of Christ is not a fact, for He believed in and preached about Hell.

The Red Cross takes up collections for storm sufferers and victims of floods and drought. Congress passes laws and appropriates money for the relief of the distressed. A recent report of some government officials indicated a good deal of anxiety because some families were so poor that they could only attend the movies once a week and other nights must remain at home! Other social activities appeal to the tenderhearted on the basis that some children do not have as much milk to drink as others, and some do not have lunch money, and some boys do not have clubs, "older brothers" and outings as do the children of the better privileged. In fact, the term "underprivileged" is used again and again these days, as if to be "underprivileged" was the greatest of disasters.

We may well help the poor, but no want or poverty, no distress of mind or body is to be compared for a moment with the torture of the damned who go to Hell. The most awful fact is the fact of Hell and that some whom we know, who live in the same houses or go to the same schools or work in the same business or are our daily companions, will die and spend an eternity away from God, eternally unforgiven, eternally sinning, and eternally doomed. That one fact will enable you to see what God meant when He said, "He that winneth souls is wise."

If one who reads this has yet any tenderness of heart, any love for his neighbor, any of the milk of human kindness, then he will see some of the spiritual wisdom in winning souls.

I do not wonder that modernists who deny the fact of Hell, or who scoff at the idea of literal fire, do not win souls. Not believing the Bible, which is the wisdom of God, it is not strange that they miss the wisdom of soul winning. Let him who would be wise consider the eternal doom of the lost.

Disappointments and Unhappiness
of This World

This present world is a failure, which fact is not hard to prove. That homes have failed is evidenced by the ever-mounting divorce rate. About one in every two and a half marriages ends in divorce, and many other couples live in stark tragedy and bitterness of soul.

Our jails are full of boys and girls. Suicides are high among high school teenagers, proving that both home and school have failed.

Governments have failed. They cannot put down crime. They cannot control graft. More than three-quarters of the population of the globe have been killing and being killed. Unbalanced budgets, mounting taxes, show the failure of the governments of the world. And disease, suicide, crime; heartless, conscienceless wickedness everywhere prove the failure of this present civilization. It is a sad, bitter, wicked world, and it offers no peace to the human heart.

I am impressed more and more with the sad, stark tragedy that stares out of the faces of people. As I preach, and the faces of people relax into the grim, sad, lonely lines of despair, I realize that this world has wrought tragedy in the heart of every person who ever put his hope in it.

Youth starts out so gay, so optimistic, with so many delightful prospects, with visions, dreams, air castles, laughter and high ambitions; but before youth merges into mature manhood or womanhood, life has become a grim business of making ends meet, or wringing some drops of joy out of the fleeting pleasures of a day. And old age comes on to bring, in most cases, a sadder disillusionment, which results either in the bitter, querulous resentment of the aged or the calmer resignation of defeat.

This is a sad, bitter, wicked, disappointing world. It does not give men and women, boys and girls what they cry out for, what they hunger for, what they need!

Here, then, is a weighty argument for winning souls. The Gospel of Jesus Christ is the only sure road to peace!

One Sunday night a young man stood in my service during the invitation time and said to a friend, "I have given up hope of ever being happy." This friend said to him, "There is no real happiness except in Jesus Christ!" Peace, soul peace, real rest for the weary and heavy laden, can be found only in Jesus Christ! You may give your wealth to the poor, you may die a martyr in a good cause, you may relieve human distress and earn the gratitude of millions; but no philanthropist ever did so much for any man as he who told him the Gospel and taught him to trust in Jesus and obtain peace of heart and forgiveness of sins!

The pleasure, the wealth and all the good things that

this world can give, fail men. How important, then, to offer troubled, sinning people the soul peace that comes with salvation! If you will be wise, remind people of the words of Jesus:

"Come unto me, all ye that labour and are heavy laden, and I will give you rest. Take my yoke upon you, and learn of me; for I am meek and lowly in heart: and ye shall find rest unto your souls. For my yoke is easy, and my burden is light."—Matt. 11:28–30.

Here is reason enough for winning souls and proof that he that winneth souls is wise.

Sufferings of Christ

What weighty reasons there are for winning souls! What crushing arguments prove the wisdom of the soul-winner's course! I press on your mind another and per-haps the most compelling of all reasons for winning souls! The sufferings of Christ prove the eternal worth of a soul.

The modernist doubts a literal Hell and the eternal torment of the unsaved. Very naturally so, for the mod-ernist doubts that the blood of Jesus Christ was shed as the only possible atonement for man's sin. But he who believes the Bible must see in the sufferings of Christ how greatly He valued a soul and how wise with the wisdom of God is the winner of souls.

The torture of Jesus by the Roman soldiers, by the mob and by wicked Jewish leaders preceding and during the crucifixion was hellish with all the venom of Satan. Unless there were some immeasurable profit to be gained, some infinite good to be bought by the sufferings of Christ, then His life and death were the folly of Jesus and the wickedness of God! If Christ does not keep souls out of torment and purchase for them eternal happiness, then He died like a fool. If by the offering of His Son, God the Father did not redeem men from the torments of Hell to everlasting life, then to put the lovely and innocent Jesus on the cross was the most awful wickedness! Oh, the death of Christ proves the worth of a soul!

Christian, if you can go through the Garden of Gethsemane with Jesus to win a soul, then you are learning a little of the wisdom of God. If, like Paul, you can bear in your body the marks of the Lord Jesus to win a soul, then you are learning the lesson of eternal wisdom which will bring the eternal fruit of joy.

John 3:16 proves the worth of a soul. Jesus' thirty-odd years away from the angels, homesick for Heaven, the poorest of the poor, 'despised and rejected,' 'a man of sorrows and acquainted with grief,' setting His face like a flint toward the cross—that is concrete evidence of how important saving a soul is and how wise is the soul winner. The sufferings of Christ for sinners form one of the best arguments for soul winning. If you would be wise like Jesus, then win souls, for that was the supreme passion of His heart.

This is what He meant when He said, "For the Son of man is come to seek and to save that which was lost" (Luke 19:10).

Glories of Heaven

At the beginning of this chapter, I indicated that true wisdom takes the long look. Proverbs commands the improvident, "Go to the ant, thou sluggard; consider her ways, and be wise," because the ant provides for tomorrow. So with the soul winner. He must somehow forget today in order to provide joy for many a tomorrow. Soul winning does not pay much in United States dollars.

The soul winner has many blessed rewards in this world. He has the great joy of the Holy Spirit's conscious presence, for no one ever won souls without an enduement from Heaven. He has the joy of answered prayer, for whoever won souls without beseeching God for wisdom and power? It is sweet to know that God has heard, and to have the burden lifted after long pleading. The soul winner enjoys the gratitude of those he wins. I remember with glad heart the affectionate thanks I have received from many I have won to Christ. I treasure a great number of letters written out of a heart full of gratitude and love by those I was privileged to snatch as brands from the burning with the Gospel of Christ.

The soul winner has much joy in this world, I say, and "he that winneth souls is wise," very largely because he believes the Word of God and knows that there will be rewards commensurate with the importance of the task—rewards in the world to come.

This is the meaning of Daniel 12:3, "And they that be wise shall shine as the brightness of the firmament; and they that turn many to righteousness as the stars for ever and ever." The rewards of the soul winner are eternal.

The man who works day and night in acquiring a fortune may wake up someday to find the fortune gone overnight. Even if he can hold it in the clutch of his withered hand, finally the monster Death will drag him away unwillingly, and his riches will slip between his palsied fingers. Men do not carry their wealth into the grave.

The fame of this world is hard won, and a man may lose in a week or a year what he has toiled for during a lifetime.

President Wilson earned the plaudits and praise of the civilized world, and sat on the highest pinnacle of fame when he went to Paris to dictate the terms of worldwide peace. Christian gentleman, idealist, statesman and orator, he held for a moment the limelight of the world. But a few months later he died a brokenhearted, disillusioned man, defeated by his opponents, forsaken by former friends, broken in health and neglected. It is well that he could say, "I am willing to wait for the verdict of mankind," for certainly the sweetness of fame had turned to wormwood and gall.

Fame of Earth

How easy it is to illustrate the vanity of fame! President Hoover was swept into office by the most overwhelming vote this nation had ever seen. But after only four years in office, he was denied a second term and was crowded out by the even more crushing victory of Franklin D. Roosevelt. The rewards that men slave for, scheme for, yea, even sometimes sell their souls for, are rewards that flee away and are found no more, like the dew that melts in the heat of the rising sun.

But not so the eternal rewards of a soul winner. He shall shine "as the brightness of the firmament," and "as the stars for ever and ever," says the Word of God.

Jesus Himself took the long look. Nothing could possibly have happened in the years of Christ's ministry that could pay Him for the loss of coming to earth and the torture of the cross. But in Isaiah 53:11 we are told that "he

shall see of the travail of his soul, and shall be satisfied."
Well did Jesus with heavenly wisdom know that all the
travail of His soul, the pouring out of His soul unto death,
would be paid for later, "when the saints go marching in."
Jesus knew that, though He had made Himself poor for
our sakes, one day the riches of the universe would be His
to enjoy again as the Creator of them all. He was despised
and rejected, but well He knew that one day He would be
crowned King of kings and Lord of lords, and rule the
nations with a rod of iron. He knew that all the Father
gave Him would one day be His, so He was content.

Jesus, then, is the great pattern for soul winners.
Concerning this, Hebrews 12:1, 2 tells us:

> *"Wherefore seeing we also are compassed about
> with so great a cloud of witnesses, let us lay aside
> every weight, and the sin which doth so easily beset
> us, and let us run with patience the race that is set
> before us, Looking unto Jesus the author and finisher
> of our faith; who for the joy that was set before him
> endured the cross, despising the shame, and is set
> down at the right hand of the throne of God."*

The inspired writer of Hebrews tells us that, for the joy
that was set before Him, Jesus endured the cross and
despised the shame. He looked forward to the joy in
Heaven, so He despised the shame of the cross and endured
it gladly. The soul winner must have the same wisdom.

I well know that the course of a soul winner will not
bring me the wealth of this world. I once thought that if I
won many souls I would gain the fame and honor of
Christian people everywhere. Alas, I find that is not true.
The churches honor the scholar more than the soul win-

ner. In denominational councils the man who can raise money for schools and hospitals is more valued than he who can keep the drunkard and the harlot out of Hell. The pay of the world for soul winning is not large. But, thank God, I can take the "long look," as Moses did when he led the children of Israel out of Egypt and was content not to be called Pharaoh's daughter's son, or be like Paul who gave up his place as a blameless Pharisee, a leader of the Sanhedrin at Jerusalem, and became the despised but soul-winning apostle to the Gentiles. Moses had insupportable burdens. Paul so suffered that he said, "If in this life only we have hope in Christ, we are of all men most miserable." Both endured as seeing Him who is invisible. They knew there is a life beyond the grave, when the soul winner will have his payday. "He that winneth souls is wise," and there will be eternal glories and rewards for the one who has the wisdom to turn many to righteousness.

My Christian friends, if the cost of soul winning seems too great, then I urge you to take private lessons from the Holy Spirit, for I Corinthians 2:14 tells us, "But the natural man receiveth not the things of the Spirit of God: for they are foolishness unto him: neither can he know them, because they are spiritually discerned." The Holy Spirit can show you the things of God, the worth of a soul, and help you to be a soul winner. No one ever wins souls except by the power of the Holy Spirit. Do not be deceived by the foolish wisdom of this world.

> *"For the preaching of the cross is to them that perish foolishness; but unto us which are saved it is the power of God....It pleased God by the foolishness of preaching to save them that believe."*— I Cor. 1:18, 21.

Let those who would be wise win souls; and when the soul winner hears the word of the Saviour, "Well done, thou good and faithful servant: thou hast been faithful over a few things, I will make thee ruler over many things: enter thou into the joy of thy lord," then he will have just begun to enjoy the eternal rewards and the glorious returns of his investments.

"He that winneth souls is wise"!

God's Way in Soul Winning

"He that goeth forth and weepeth, bearing precious seed, shall doubtless come again with rejoicing, bringing his sheaves with him."—Ps. 126:6.

Soul winning is the main job of a Christian. The saving of sinners is the thing nearest to the heart of God. For that purpose Christ came to earth, lived, died and rose again. Even now the angels in Heaven rejoice more over one sinner that repents than over ninety-nine just persons who need no repentance. Soul winning is the eternal business. One sows now, then reaps throughout the endless ages of glory.

How may I win souls? should be the chief concern of every child of God. The Scripture says, "Let him that heareth say, Come." And the Great Commission is given to every Christian. He is to go into all the world and make disciples.

The Bible has much to say about how to win souls. Here in Psalm 126:6, God's way of winning souls is clearly laid out. A meditation on this passage, directed by the Holy Spirit, should certainly make clear God's infallible method in the winning of souls.

This is a psalm of revival:

*"When the Lord turned again the captivity of
Zion, we were like them that dream. Then was our
mouth filled with laughter, and our tongue with
singing: then said they among the heathen, The
Lord hath done great things for them. The Lord
hath done great things for us; whereof we are
glad. Turn again our captivity, O Lord, as the
streams in the south. They that sow in tears shall
reap in joy. He that goeth forth and weepeth, bearing precious seed, shall doubtless come again with
rejoicing, bringing his sheaves with him."*

"When the Lord turned again the captivity of Zion, we
were like them that dream." The captivity referred to
must be the Babylonian captivity. We do not know the
author of this psalm, but we know it is inspired by God.
David wrote many psalms. Solomon, Moses, Asaph and
others wrote some. The inspired writer here recalls the
happy revival when the remnant under Nehemiah and
Ezra returned from Babylon to build again the walls of
Jerusalem and the Temple. It seemed too good to be
true—it was almost like a happy dream when God turned
the captivity of Zion.

Then their mouths were filled with happy laughter. It
was not frivolous laughter, but the deep, joyous laughter so close to tears, so close to the shouting of praise. I
have never yet broken out into uncontrollable shouting
of praise, but sometimes I have been so happy that I
could not refrain from laughter. Sarah must have felt so
when God gave her the promised boy in her old age and
she called him Isaac, "Laughter!" Many of us look back
with mingled joy and longing to the times of great
revival and blessing, when our mouths were filled with

laughter and our tongues with singing.

"Then said they among the heathen, The Lord hath done great things for them. The Lord hath done great things for us; whereof we are glad." The heathen were impressed with the marvelous deliverance which God gave His people. Real, Heaven-sent revivals are like that. Outsiders know when God has visited His people. A great moving of repentance among the people of God, of tears, of restitution and reformation, times of joy and blessing and reconciliation, make a profound impression upon a community. Such had been the revival to which the psalmist here refers, and then his heart cries out to God for a return of revival. "Turn again our captivity, O Lord, as the streams in the south."

Beware of Spiritual Bondage

There are other captivities worse than being carried into Babylon. Our churches, our hearts, our prayers are cold. The Bible becomes a dull Book. The ministry becomes a thankless task—a burden to be borne. Our services become mere form, our songs, meaningless. We feel the parching drought of worldliness. Our souls long for a breath from Heaven. We need a rain of the Holy Spirit upon God's people. We are carried captive by our sins and are crushed by the world about us. O God, turn our captivity again!

The psalmist prays a big prayer and asks for a great revival. "Turn again our captivity, O Lord, as the streams in the south." Possibly he has in mind the Nile River, rising in Lake Tana in Ethiopia, then flowing down through the hills to the broad plains of Egypt, where every year, until conquered by the British dam, it overflowed all the banks and watered the lowland. It irrigated the valleys and enriched the soil with overwhelming flood tides of resistless water! May God send that kind of revival! As the song says,

Mercy drops round us are falling,
But for the showers we plead.

Or the psalmist may have had in mind the Euphrates and Tigris Rivers, great broad streams that flow together and then sweep majestically on southeastward to empty their mighty burden into the Persian Gulf. We need to pray, expect and try to have revivals that are as mighty as "the streams in the south."

"They that sow in tears shall reap in joy," the Scripture says.

Revivals and soul winning are always matters of sowing and reaping. It costs to be a soul winner. Soul winning should be a matter of the deepest concern. If a soul winner is willing to sow in tears, he will certainly be able to reap in joy.

In verse 6, we have a clear outline of God's way to win souls and the certainty of results: "He that goeth forth and weepeth, bearing precious seed, shall doubtless come again with rejoicing, bringing his sheaves with him."

Analyze that verse and you will find these five parts in God's plan of soul winning:

1. "He that goeth forth"—the GO in soul winning.

2. "And weepeth"—the BROKEN HEART in soul winning.

3. "Bearing precious seed"—the WORD OF GOD in soul winning.

4. "Shall doubtless come again...bringing his sheaves

with him"—the CERTAINTY OF RESULTS with God's method.

5. "Rejoicing...bringing his sheaves with him"—the JOY OF THE REAPERS, or a soul-winner's reward.

The "Go" in Soul Winning

God's Word puts going as the first requirement in soul winning. How like the Great Commission, when Jesus said, "Go ye into all the world" (Mark 16:15), and again, "Go ye therefore" (Matt. 28:19). The main reason Christians do not win souls is that they simply do not get at it. The one who wins souls is the one who tries to win souls, the one who talks to sinners, the one who makes it his business.

Many have the impression that the best man or woman is the best soul winner—that the Christian who has the highest moral standards, pays his debts, avoids worldliness, attends church, tithes, etc., will automatically be the best soul winner. If it were true, then every Pharisee would have been a wonderful soul winner, but they were not. And many a Christian today prays, reads his Bible, attends church and carefully watches his daily life, yet never wins a soul. That is tragic but true.

How often in revivals a good sister or brother rises to testify and says, "I want to live such a godly life that sinners will see my daily walk and be saved!" The fact is, living a godly life is not the way God has appointed to get sinners saved. Living a good life is vitally important for the one who would be a soul winner, but the first condition of soul winning, divinely appointed, is this— get up and go after sinners!

Soul winners ought to know the Bible, but the best

Bible students are often not the best soul winners. Many, many times in revivals I have noticed that preachers would sit in the services, enjoy the sermons, pray in public and show an active interest, but would win very few sinners to Christ. But in the same revival I have seen a young person who had not been long converted, who knew little about the Bible and had little time to grow in Christian grace, yet who persistently and earnestly went after his friends until he won far more souls than the preachers. I have known a fifteen-year-old girl to win more souls in a revival than a half-dozen sincere preachers, and the reason was that she obeyed the command of the Scriptures to go after that which was lost.

If you want to be a soul winner, the first thing to do is to "go!"

I have known mothers and fathers to see their unsaved children grow up in the midst of prayers, Bible reading and moral teaching, yet never once earnestly, lovingly and persistently press an immediate decision for Christ. Among the hundreds of sinners I have dealt with, no cases are sadder than the unsaved sons and daughters of ministers. Young people tell me how they were accustomed to family prayer in the home, how they believed with all their heart in the sincerity of mother's and father's faith; yet it would seem that neither ever went after his or her children for definite and immediate decision. There is no possible substitute for the "go" in soul winning. Doubtless Paul was the greatest of all the apostles, and his greatness lay most of all in that he was "in labours more abundant."

Soul winning is not a matter of talent. People do not win souls because they are educated or are peculiarly fitted for it by nature or have magnetic personalities. Those who win the most souls are those who most persistently and with the greatest abandon go after sinners.

We must realize that soul winning is not done in human power and wisdom but the power of the Holy Spirit convicts and converts a sinner. But remember that Jesus said, "Go . . . and, lo, I am with you alway, even unto the end of the world" (Matt. 28:19, 20). The obedient heart who sets about the Master's business, obeying His plain command to win souls, is far more likely to have the power of the Holy Spirit upon him. Going is God's first requirement for soul winning.

One who would win souls must "be instant in season, out of season" (II Tim. 4:2). The best soul winners are those who go when it is and when it is not convenient. "Blessed are ye that sow beside all waters" (Isa. 32:20) is just another way of saying, "Blessed is the soul winner who tries to reach every sinner possible." Again, "He that observeth the wind shall not sow; and he that regardeth the clouds shall not reap" (Eccles. 11:4).

You may think you do not know enough Scripture, but in a few minutes you can learn John 3:16, and that has led to thousands of conversions. Learn it and go. You may feel you do not know what to say. Ask God to give you the message and go! You may not know to whom you should speak, but if in loving obedience you go, the Holy Spirit will direct your steps and your words. "He that goeth forth" is the one who will win souls.

It is said that in the last years of the war between the states, a farmer was drafted into the Confederate army. He did not know the drill manual, did not know how to keep step on the march, nor how to salute. Nor did he know any of the bugle calls. But he brought his squirrel rifle, and when the command was given to attack, he charged the Yankee lines, joining in the rebel yell. However, the gray-coated Confederates were outnumbered and were soon driven back. The bugle blew "retreat," and the thin gray line withdrew to safer ground.

As the battered soldiers treated their wounded, prepared their camp and threw up breastworks in the late afternoon, someone said, "Poor old Jim! He was either killed or taken prisoner in the first battle he was ever in! Too bad he didn't know the bugle call to retreat and ran right into that nest of Yankees."

But about sundown they saw two tired fellows coming over the hill. The one in front had on a blue uniform and the man behind wore a gray. Somebody had taken a prisoner! As he saw the camp, he prodded his prisoner with a bayonet and somebody shouted, "It is Jim! Jim's got a prisoner! Where did you get him, Jim?" The farmer recruit drew up angrily. He felt they had all deserted him in the first battle! "Where did I get him?" he said. "Why, the woods are full of them! Why don't you get one yourself?"

The world is full of sinners, and you can take them alive for Christ, if only you will go after them.

Somewhere near you is a poor, lost soul, someone who would listen to you, someone who is burdened, someone who realizes he needs Christ. That soul is not saved because nobody has gone to tell him the message of salvation.

"Go" is the first command of God to the soul winner. "He that goeth forth" is the man who returns with sheaves. If you want to be a soul winner, then commit yourself to this holy business and go after sinners. Other things are necessary, but this is most necessary. If you would be a winner of souls, then you must go forth.

The Broken Heart in Soul Winning

"He that goeth forth and weepeth," the psalmist says, will come back with sheaves, rejoicing. Beyond all doubt, this is another essential for the soul winner. If going forth is the first requirement of a soul winner, perhaps even the going involves a broken heart. If we care as we ought, we will go. A broken heart will send us forth.

It is amazing that we have few tears when there is so much to weep about. Have you ever felt the compassion that Jesus had as He looked on the multitude? Have you ever experienced what was in His heart as He wept over Jerusalem, and said, "O Jerusalem, Jerusalem, thou that killest the prophets, and stonest them which are sent unto thee, how often would I have gathered thy children together, even as a hen gathereth her chickens under her wings, and ye would not!"? The love of the shepherd for the lost sheep, the tender compassion of the father for his prodigal son, exemplify the broken heart of God and of Christ over sinners. To win souls, we must go, weeping.

Sometimes preachers are ashamed to weep; more often our hearts are too cold to weep over sinners. It was not so with Paul. To the assembled elders of Ephesus, he urgently said, "Therefore watch, and remember, that by the space of three years I ceased not to warn every one night and day with tears" (Acts 20:31). Paul warned people night and day. In verse 20 of the same chapter, he declares that he taught "publickly, and from house to house." He put the "go" in soul winning. But best of all, he went with tears! The one who will come back rejoicing with sheaves is he who sows in tears.

Often I am amazed at the callousness of my own heart. How strangely absorbed we become in the things about us until we have little concern about souls—to be eternally blessed or to be eternally tormented!

> **Would you care if some friend**
> **You had met day by day**
> **Should never be told about Jesus?**
> **Are you willing that he**
> **In the judgment should say,**
> **"No one ever told me of Jesus"?**

When I first began preaching, I remember how I wept. I was embarrassed about it. This was wholly unlike the college debating, the commencement addresses and other public speaking to which I had been accustomed. The tears flowed down my cheeks almost continually, and I was so broken up that sometimes I could scarcely talk.

Then I grew ashamed of my tears and longed to speak more logically. As I recall, I asked the Lord to give me better control of myself as I preached. My tears soon vanished, and I found I had only the dry husk of preaching left. Then I begged God to give me again the broken heart, the concern, even if it meant tears in public, and a trembling voice.

I feel the same need today. We preachers ought to cry out like Jeremiah, "Oh that my head were waters, and mine eyes a fountain of tears, that I might weep day and night for the slain of the daughter of my people!" (Jer. 9:1).

The personal soul winner needs a broken heart. The cold and callous sinner can, it may be, answer all your arguments and withstand all your pleas, but he has no argument against tears. If you have a holy compassion given of God and wrought by the Holy Spirit in your heart, until tears flow down your face as you talk to sinners, then you have a magnet that must tug at the heart of the coldest and hardest of unbelievers. After all, nothing can prove you and your message better than a love like Christ had for sinners. It is not hard to believe that God so loved the world, that He gave His Son, if those of us who tell about it have some of the same love to transform our appeal and give urgency to our message. May God give us tears!

Do You Care for the Dying?

Humanly speaking, there must be a multitude who are unsaved because no one especially cares. Many a man has felt in his heart the cry of the psalmist, "No man cared for my soul!"

A college senior told me, weeping, after I had just won him to Christ, "Nobody seemed to care whether I was saved or not!" One of the standing complaints that the sinner and the backslider have against our modern churches is that, when they go to church, no one seems to care. No one shakes hands with them, no one seems glad to see them.

A seventeen-year-old boy in Waxahachie, Texas, told Mrs. Rice that no one had ever in his life talked to him about being a Christian. His mother and father were church members, he had often attended Sunday school and church and revivals, yet no one had ever urged him to trust Christ and be saved. Surely it must have been that no one cared very much.

Several years ago I lived in Ft. Worth on Seminary Hill, and made that my headquarters as an evangelist. In the Southwestern Baptist Theological Seminary located there, I had taken my training. Mrs. Rice and I often attended the Seminary Hill Baptist Church (now the Gambrell Street Baptist Church). She attended a class for women taught by Mrs. Scarborough, a fine teacher, whose illustrious husband had been president of the seminary for many years. He was a great soul winner, an earnest man of God, and his wife a blessed, good Christian.

In the class was an unsaved woman. My wife became concerned about her and said to me one day, "Will you go with me to see this lost woman and try to win her?" I agreed to go, but with a great deal of anxiety. She lived among preachers. Her next-door neighbor on one side was a preacher, I think; on the other side lived a Christian educational worker. Three or four doors away lived the president of the seminary. I lived not far away, and so did many other preachers. This unsaved woman had been attending the services. I felt that surely she must be gospel-hardened. It seemed to me likely that she had been approached many, many times about her soul in that warm evangelistic atmosphere.

With some dread we prepared to go visit her and try to win her to Christ. My wife engaged a woman to stay with the children a whole afternoon, and after prayer we went to call on the unsaved woman, prepared for a long and hard battle to win her to Christ.

She met us at the door with a friendly smile. She seemed pleased that we had come to see her. We are so often cowards when we come to speak about Christ, and that afternoon I looked about me to find some point of contact that I might come gradually to the question of salvation. On the table I saw a nice new Bible, and I commented upon it.

She said, "Yes, my mother gave me that last Christmas."

Then I said, "I understand you are not a Christian. Wouldn't it be wonderful if you were a Christian, so that you and your husband could read the Word of God together every night?"

Her face was very grave as she answered, "We are not Christians, but we do read the Bible every night. Every night since last Christmas we have read a chapter in this new Bible."

Somewhat taken back and nonplused, I started over again. "But if you were a Christian, you and your husband could get down together and ask God to bless you and lead you right and keep you safe through the night. Wouldn't it be fine to be a Christian and have family prayer?"

Tears came into her eyes as she said, "I'm not a Christian, but we do pray. Every night my husband and I read a chapter in this Bible, then get down on our knees and pray."

I hardly knew what to say. Here was a woman whom I had supposed was gospel-hardened. I supposed that many, many times she had turned down the Saviour. Living in the midst of Christians and special workers, I thought that surely she must have been urged many times to trust in Christ. But instead of being hardened, she and her husband were daily reading the Bible and praying. And even then she was in tears!

So I left off all devices and plainly asked the question, "Then why is it that you have turned down Jesus? Why is it you are not a Christian?"

Breaking out into sobbing she said, "I want to be a Christian, but I don't know how!"

My heart was stirred. To my shame I found that right

here, a few blocks away from me, was a woman who daily read the Bible and prayed and tried to find God. Around her were preachers and their wives and others dedicated to lifetime Christian work as gospel singers, Christian education workers and missionaries. All of us were occupied with our own affairs and never took time to tell this lost woman how to be saved.

I took up the new Bible and said, "Well, God bless you; you are going to find out how to be saved." I turned to the third chapter of John and read the wonderful story about how one must be born again, how God loves sinners, and how those who believe in Christ have everlasting life and shall never perish. In five minutes she was a happy, rejoicing Christian.

This incident has come back to my mind many times to remind me of this question, "Do you really care about sinners?" We are so professional, so formal, that we let people all around us go to Hell. If we had a broken heart over sinners, if we went forth weeping to find those who need the Saviour, we would feel responsible to find out who was lost.

Many are hardhearted and indifferent. Many do not want to discuss their sad, lost condition. But if we go 'with tears and hearts full of tender love for sinners for whom Jesus died, we will find those who can be won.

How shameful it will be for many Christians when they hear the plaintive cry of lost sinners at the judgment of God, "No man cared for my soul"! (Ps. 142:4). I know that all who reject Christ are without excuse. Men ought to seek the Saviour and find Him, for He is not far from every penitent heart. But I know also that any Christian who does not love and seek sinners is also without excuse.

He is untrue to His Saviour, ungrateful for his own salvation, and disobedient to the Great Commission that God has given him.

May God give us tender, broken hearts and weeping eyes as we go out to win souls.

Tears touch the heart of God. He said to Hezekiah, "I have heard thy prayer, I have seen thy tears: behold, I will add unto thy days fifteen years" (Isa. 38:5). If tears touch the heart of God, we may be sure they make a way into the hardest hearts. Nothing proves a soul-winner's sincerity like his broken heart, his tearful concern. I know that there is a difference in my preaching when God gives me a heavenly compassion for sinners, until I yearn over them in the tenderest, brokenhearted anxiety.

"He that goeth forth and weepeth" is the man who will come back rejoicing with his sheaves. The broken heart is indispensable for the soul winner. And if you do not have a broken heart, a concern for sinners, and tears over their lost condition, then I suggest that you wait before God until the Holy Spirit gives you this Christlike concern, this shepherd heart to seek the lost ones. Wait before the Lord until He gives you tears out of His boundless, world-embracing, brokenhearted love for sinners; then go forth.

The Word of God in Soul Winning

The soul winner must go forth not only weeping, but "bearing precious seed." In the parable of the sower, the Saviour tells us, "The seed is the word of God" (Luke 8:11). This is the precious seed that the soul winner must carry if he is to come back with sheaves.

How important it is that we take the good seed, the only seed that has the divine power to spring up in the

human heart with the fruit of salvation! The would-be
soul winner must know ahead of time that he cannot win
souls by human wisdom, human influence, personal magnetism or tact. He goes not to reform men, but to save
them. A reformation might take place without a supernatural, divine act in the heart. Men have been known to
leave off drinking, cursing, or even a career of crime,
under the moral influence of some strong character or
some great life. But that is not salvation. Unless there is a
supernatural change of heart, a regeneration, a new birth,
the sinner is still a lost sinner, a rejecter of Christ, a rebel
against God, justly condemned and Hell-bound.

Dear soul winner, you must have heavenly help in this
business of saving sinners. "For the weapons of our warfare are not carnal, but mighty through God to the pulling
down of strong holds" (II Cor. 10:4). You must take
supernatural weapons for this warfare, supernatural seed
for this sowing. You must take the living, supernatural
Word of God. "For the word of God is quick, and powerful, and sharper than any twoedged sword, piercing even
to the dividing asunder of soul and spirit, and of the joints
and marrow, and is a discerner of the thoughts and
intents of the heart" (Heb. 4:12). Remember the word of
God to Jeremiah: "Is not my word like as a fire? saith the
Lord; and like a hammer that breaketh the rock in
pieces?" (Jer. 23:29).

Depend upon the Word of God to bring conviction.
You cannot outtalk a sinner. Do not depend upon long,
drawn-out arguments. Place your dependence upon the
sharp Word of God. This is holy seed and within every
verse there is the germ of eternal life. The soul winner
must have confidence in the living Word of God. It is

inspired of God. The Word of God reveals every sinner's condition. It shows the love of God. Its promises are so faithful that faith comes by hearing the Word of God. If you go forth weeping, sowing this seed, you may expect a blessed harvest.

The soul winner ought to learn by memory many Scriptures. He should saturate himself in the message of the Word of God. He should speak in terms of the Word. He should surrender himself to the Holy Spirit who is the Author of the Word. When the Spirit wields the Sword of the Spirit, then a mighty work is done.

Often, some wife has said, "O Brother Rice, I hope you can say something that will touch my husband's heart." Let us not think that illustrations, logic, songs or poems will win souls. These are useful and blessed of God only as they carry the Word, and as they shed light and understanding upon the Word of God. Blessed is the soul winner who quotes a Scripture, or better yet, who points out a suitable verse to a sinner and has him read it. There are Scriptures to fit every case, and the well-prepared, Spirit-led soul winner will use the Word of God with mighty effect.

Once in our home a group agreed to pray while a young woman went to see a lost girl friend. We prayed until we were assured that God had heard; then I went to find the young woman. I found the lost girl standing in a kitchen door looking at John 5:24 in a Testament held open before her face by the Christian young woman.

As it dawned upon her that by simply receiving Christ she could have everlasting life and never lose it, the dear girl said, "Oh, I never knew that was in the Bible; I did not know it was as easy as that!" Tearfully, she trusted the Saviour, and all of us rejoiced together. The Word of God did the work.

Dear soul winner, as you go and weep over sinners, take with you the precious Word of God, the seed, the power of God unto salvation to everyone who believes.

The Certainty of Results

The Scripture says, "He that goeth forth and weepeth, bearing precious seed, shall doubtless come again with rejoicing, bringing his sheaves with him." There is a certainty about results when we go in God's way. God's plans are infallible. Anybody can be a soul winner, if he is willing to go in the way God has laid out here in His Word. The word "doubtless" here means without any doubt.

You may have to plead with ten sinners to win one, or with a hundred to win ten, or with a thousand to win a hundred. When the sower of whom Jesus spoke went forth to sow, some seed fell by the wayside and was carried away by the birds, without sprouting. I know that many sinners will never listen seriously to the Gospel. Satan takes the seed out of the heart before it has time to take root. Other seed fell among stones. Some hearts are too hard, it seems, for the Word of God to take any permanent root. In other sad cases where people receive the Word it is so choked by the cares of this world and the deceitfulness of riches that it brings no fruit to perfection. We need not expect every sinner we talk to will be saved. But, thank God, some seed will fall in good soil and bring forth fruit, some thirty, some sixty and some an hundredfold.

Did you ever "drop corn" on the farm? If so, you planted two, three, or four grains in each hill. Only one good stalk of corn is desired in a hill, but a crow may get one seed and a cutworm another, and some seed will not sprout. So to insure a good stand, one must use more seed than he expects to come to full fruitage.

The cotton planter plants cotton seed thickly in a row, and when it comes up it is thinned out to a proper stand. Not every seed comes to mature fruitage, but the one who uses plenty of good seed makes a crop.

The soul winner will have disappointments. We will never win all the lost. "Wide is the gate, and broad is the way, that leadeth to destruction, and many there be which go in thereat" (Matt. 7:13). More people will be lost than will be saved. We will never get the world converted. But the soul winner who goes forth weeping, bearing precious seed, will snatch some brands from the burning. He will come back with his sheaves.

If you go out to seek lost people, you will find some are not at home, and others will not listen. A thousand hindrances will prevent the consummation of your purpose. But where one family has moved, you will find another with lost members. Where one will not hear, you will find somebody else eager for the message. You may have to turn from the rich to the poor, from the merry to the sad, before you find a willing audience for your message. You may have to turn from your own loved ones to find a stranger. If those about you will not hear, you may have to go to those in the hospitals and jails. But you may be sure that "he that goeth forth and weepeth, bearing precious seed," shall certainly come back with souls. It will take going, it will take a broken heart, and it will take the life-giving Word of God; but this combination never fails.

Going forth with weeping, sowing for the Master,
   Though the loss sustained our spirit often grieves;
When our weeping's over, He will bid us welcome,
   We shall come rejoicing, bringing in the sheaves.

The Soul Winner's Joy

When one goes forth and weeps, and bears precious seed and comes back with sheaves, then how fitting that divine inspiration should say he shall "doubtless come again with rejoicing, bringing his sheaves with him"!

There is no joy like the soul winner's joy. The shepherd who comes home with the one lost sheep "calleth together his friends and neighbours, saying unto them, Rejoice with me; for I have found my sheep which was lost." The woman who loses a piece of silver and finds it "calleth her friends and her neighbours together, saying, Rejoice with me; for I have found the piece which I had lost." And when the Prodigal Son comes back to the father, they kill the fatted calf and the home is marked by a feasting and rejoicing over the boy which "was dead, and is alive again...lost, and is found."

So we are told that "likewise joy shall be in heaven over one sinner that repenteth, more than over ninety and nine just persons, which need no repentance"; and again, "Likewise, I say unto you, there is joy in the presence of the angels of God over one sinner that repenteth." It is only fitting that they that sow in tears should reap in joy. So when we share the compassionate heart of the Saviour, God allows us to share the joy which is in the presence of the angels. It was the soul winner's joy that Jesus had in mind when He was willing to die for sinners. He "for the joy that was set before Him endured the cross, despising the shame" (Heb. 12:2). He had in mind the joy of reaping.

In the marvelous fifty-third chapter of Isaiah, where we are told that Jesus would bear our iniquities and that with His stripes we should be healed, because He would pour out His soul unto death, we are also told that "He shall see of the travail of his soul, and shall be satisfied." Therefore, the Lord Jesus will come rejoicing, bringing in the sheaves, and all that have had a part in the sowing and a share in His weeping will rejoice with Him "when the saints go marching in." When 'many shall come from the east and west, and shall sit down with Abraham, and Isaac, and Jacob in the kingdom of heaven,' what a time of rejoicing that will be for all who sowed the precious seed and watered it with tears!

Others have the fame and plaudits of this world. Let Congress make the laws; let vulgar and immoral movie stars have the limelight on TV and in the nation's press; but when the soul winner comes back with the drunkard, saved and made sober, or with the harlot made pure or even with a little child transformed by being born again, the soul winner has the best of the bargain. And if we catch some gleams of joy here in the midst of our weeping, what a joyful reaping when the Saviour comes and gathers up His jewels and we see for the first time the fullness of our reaping!

The soul winner must take the long look, and by faith look forward to the time when he will be paid a hundredfold for all his tears, all his sorrows, all his self-denials.

If you are defeated, discontented, unhappy; if you have lost the joy of the Lord and you do not enjoy prayer and the Bible and Christian service as you once did, then you need to give yourself with a holy abandon to going after sinners, weeping, bearing precious seed. When you come back, as you doubtless will, with sheaves, then you will come with rejoicing. Lost joy will be restored to the Christian who wins souls.

Just now the morning mail comes and with it a letter, enclosing a copy of my booklet, *What Must I Do to Be Saved?* with a decision slip signed. The man who signs his name as taking Christ as his personal Saviour says in the letter, "This pamphlet was handed to me by Mr. F. W. W; he insisted that I read every word, which I did." Just now I feel part of the joy I have been talking about over a sinner's getting saved. There is no joy like coming back with sheaves.

Here is God's way of winning souls, and here are the divinely appointed results, so let us put in practice this precious verse: "He that goeth forth and weepeth, bearing precious seed, shall doubtless come again with rejoicing, bringing his sheaves with him."

The Compassionate Heart

"They that sow in tears shall reap in joy."—Ps. 126:5.

Hear these remarkable words, "In tears!" The tears of a broken heart are necessary equipment of the soul winner. The certainty of returning with joy depends, says Holy Writ, on going with tears. There are other requirements for the one who would be a fisher of men. He must go, he must bear precious seed, but the thing so often lacking is the broken heart. Indeed, I make bold to say that it is the broken heart that drives one out, that makes him go. The broken heart will sow the seed that will bring forth fruit. Yea, even the same broken heart will make the homecoming joyful.

There is joy in the surcease of a broken heart. The broken and compassionate heart, the humble and contrite spirit please God, attract the sinner; and the contact between these two results in the changed heart and saved soul of a sinner and brings honor to the Saviour.

See the example of Jesus. Never was there such a compassionate winner of men! He saw the people as sheep having no shepherd and "had compassion on them." He wept over Jerusalem. He sought the fallen woman to forgive her and the publican to make him a preacher. His compassion would not let Him eat. He found "meat that ye know not of" in the winning of souls. His compassionate heart would not let Him sleep, for He must needs go into a mountain and pray all night or rise a great while before day to pray for the lost. His compassionate heart would not let Him die, even, till the repenting thief on the neighboring cross was forgiven and won to Himself and Heaven. The Prodigal Son was a sinner, and the forgiving, grieving father was like Jesus. Christ was the Shepherd, and the sinner was the poor lost lamb, at the mercy of the cold and the beasts. As the shepherd seeks the sheep until he finds it, rescues it, and rejoices over it, so Jesus with the sinner.

They crowned Him with thorns,
He was beaten with stripes;
   He was smitten and nailed to the tree.
But the pain in His heart was the hardest to bear,
   The heart that was broken for me.

No marvel, then, that when He died on the cross for sinners and the soldiers opened His side with a spear, they found a heart literally broken. O Saviour, teach us to love sinners, to weep over them, to find pillows hard and food tasteless and life not worth living, if they be not saved! Send us out with compassion and tears to win the lost!

How Paul wept over sinners! Hear him say, "Remember, that by the space of three years I ceased not to warn every one night and day with tears." Night and day! Night and day with tears! Hear him say, "Brethren, my heart's desire and prayer to God for Israel is, that they might be saved." And again he said: "For I could wish that myself were accursed from Christ for my brethren, my kinsmen according to the flesh." A stoning, a shipwreck, a life-and-death fight with lions in the coliseum, a Philippian jail at midnight, with his bleeding back and shackled feet, could not quench Paul's tears for lost men nor distract his compassionate heart till they were saved.

All the great winners of men have had compassion. Moody, Spurgeon, Torrey and Finney succeeded beyond other preachers in winning souls mainly, if not solely, because of this compassion. Charles Alexander showed it in his singing. John Vassar, Bible agent, tract distributor and soul winner rare, oh, so rare, had this compassion and yet almost no equipment by nature in his personal work. No one will win souls without it. The preacher, the teacher, the everyday Christian will do well to cultivate this compassionate heart. He may have all else without the broken heart, but will not, cannot, win the lost to a Saviour who died for them.

Once there was a preacher on the streets of a Texas town who strangely stirred and melted the hearts of men in his unlettered street preaching. The people heard him gladly, and you will not marvel when you know that they called him "Weeping Joe." I do not know, nor want to know, his other name, for no other name can so well recall the tears and prayers and the heartbroken, compassionate love of Jesus which he had for a lost world.

O Saviour, give us the broken heart, that going forth, weeping, we may come again with rejoicing, bringing precious sheaves!

The Soul Winner's Fire

"For since I spake, I cried out, I cried violence and spoil; because the word of the Lord was made a reproach unto me, and a derision, daily. Then I said, I will not make mention of him, nor speak any more in his name. But his word was in mine heart as a burning fire shut up in my bones, and I was weary with forbearing, and I could not stay."—Jer. 20:8, 9.

The soul-winning testimony of a child of God depends upon fire from Heaven. Isaiah found himself totally unprepared and unable to speak for God. "I am undone," said he, "I am a man of unclean lips, and I dwell in the midst of a people of unclean lips" (Isa. 6:5). But a seraph took a coal of heavenly fire from off the altar in the Temple, touched his lips and said, "Lo, this hath touched thy lips; and thine iniquity is taken away, and thy sin purged." Then Isaiah heard the call of God and said, "Here am I; send me." No man is fit to preach nor to witness for Christ until he be touched with fire from Heaven.

Of John the Baptist, Jesus said, "He was a burning and a shining light" (John 5:35). Moses was called to his work by the God who spoke to him out of a burning bush; and that burning bush, flaming but never consumed, is a type of every prophet of God touched by a supernatural fire from God.

The fire of God fell on Mount Carmel in answer to the prayer of Elijah, and this heavenly fire was a sign to the people that Elijah was God's prophet and that his message was true. The people fell on their faces and said, "The Lord, he is the God" (I Kings 18:39).

The one hundred and twenty disciples who were filled with the Holy Ghost at Pentecost had outward, visible tongues of fire sitting upon them, symbols of the Holy Spirit as the Enduer and Anointer of His people for service.

One who would speak for Jesus needs fire from Heaven! The call, the preparation, the passion, the power of a soul winner depend upon the fire of the Holy Spirit!

How many preachers have had the experience of Jeremiah? He cried out against the wickedness of his day and warned of the judgment of God that was certain to come to Israel. But for such preaching Jeremiah was derided and reproached. In Jeremiah 20:8, he says, "For since I spake, I cried out, I cried violence and spoil; because the word of the Lord was made a reproach unto me, and a derision, daily." He was not a popular preacher—no preacher is popular if he preaches all the counsel of God. Jesus said, "Woe unto you, when all men shall speak well of you!" When Jesus was despised and ready to be crucified, He said to His disciples, "The servant is not greater than his lord."

Sometimes the burden of the ministry is almost insupportable. Under the fires of criticism that every true preacher faces, he must choose one of three courses. He can compromise, soft-pedal, use smoother words; say not so much about sin and repentance and judgment, and thus continue in the ministry without the continual harassment that was the lot of such prophets of God as Jeremiah, Elijah and Paul. Or a preacher may resign himself, as the best Bible preachers did, to suffer malice, reproach and ridicule of wicked sinners and worldly church men, and continue faithfully to preach. The third course open is to leave the ministry, which hundreds of preachers have done, not having the fortitude to face continual opposition, yet with too much conscience and honesty to compromise Christ and dilute His message.

Jeremiah Quits the Ministry

This was the case with Jeremiah. He decided to quit the ministry. In Jeremiah 20:9, we are told, "Then I said, I will not make mention of him, nor speak any more in his name."

Jeremiah had prophesied that Judah should be carried away captive for their sins (Jer. 18:15–17; 19:8, 9; 20:4–6). Besides, Jeremiah had been a "blue-law" preacher, insisting on strict observance of the Sabbath (Jer. 17:19–27). The people had agreed among themselves, "Let us not give heed to any of his words" (Jer. 18:18).

Jeremiah's prophecies about the destruction and desolation of Jerusalem aroused Pashur, a priest, chief governor of the house of the Lord. "Then Pashur smote Jeremiah the prophet, and put him in the stocks that were in the high gate of Benjamin, which was by the house of the Lord" (Jer. 20:2). Brave man of God that he was, when Jeremiah was released from the stocks, he continued to preach. But the public whipping and exposure in the stocks was followed by such derision on the part of the people that finally Jeremiah's heart was broken and he said, "I will not make mention of him, nor speak any more in his name." Jeremiah decided to leave the ministry!

Do not blame him too quickly. He was a well-born man, a priest, intelligent and cultured. This was his first great persecution. Small wonder that he decided to speak no more in the name of the Lord, but to let people go their way to destruction, with no further admonition, since they would not heed his warning.

The Fire in Jeremiah's Bones

But when Jeremiah decided not to make mention any more of the Lord, nor to speak in His name, he found a seething volcano within him, a fire shut up in his bones! He said, "I will not make mention of him, nor speak any more in his name. But his word was in mine heart as a burning fire shut up in my bones, and I was weary with forbearing, and I could not stay."

Outward circumstances and his relation to the people tempted him to quit the ministry; but inward circumstances, the fire of God upon him, would not let him stop speaking in the name of the Lord. Jeremiah was not only in the ministry; the ministry was in him! He was like the man who had the billy goat by the horns and cried, "Somebody come and help me turn this animal loose!"

There are just too many preachers who can preach or not preach, just as is convenient. They are like the "moderate drinker" who boasts of his liquor that he "can take it or leave it alone." There are too many preachers who will preach if they are well paid but will not preach without a job.

When I was a boy I was amazed that country preachers, pastors of half-time and fourth-time country churches, rarely went to their own churches to preach on the fifth Sunday of the month. They were not "employed" for that week!

And all over America are scores of men not preaching. They say they are called of God to preach and would gladly accept a paying position in the ministry, but they never preach on the street nor in the jails nor in shops or factories; never do house-to-house soul winning!

It may be there are not enough well-paying jobs for all the preachers. It may be that all who are called to preach cannot preach to large and enthusiastic audiences with the acclaim of men. But there are enough dying men to hear the message of every preacher who will tell the story of Christ and redemption. It is as true today as in the time of Jesus, that "the harvest truly is plenteous, but the labourers are few." It is still true that we should "pray ye therefore the Lord of the harvest, that he will send forth labourers into his harvest."

I have a special burden for ministers of the Gospel. The greatest problem of the churches is the preacher problem. "Like priest, like people." Our preachers are usually good men, often learned men, unselfish, self-sacrificing, sincere men; but that is not enough. Preachers lack the divine fire, the Christ-like passion, the John the Baptist boldness, the Pauline urgency, the Holy Spirit enduement of power that will fire the churches of God. They lack the supernatural evidences that accompanied New Testament preachers.

The miraculous, the supernatural is missing in the average preacher's life and message and results. God have pity on us! What all of us need and must have to please God and do His work effectively is the fire in our bones that Jeremiah had.

We have depended on culture and learning, but schools and literature do not make prophets like Jeremiah! We have depended on organizations and institutions, but they do not bring the power that came at Pentecost and converted 3,000 souls in a day. Our colleges and seminaries send out preachers; but do the same signs and wonders attend them as were shown in the ministry of Barnabas and Saul, who went out, "being sent forth by the Holy Ghost" (Acts 13:4), with a miraculous, supernatural commission, with explicit instructions that came during fasting and prayer, with the miracle-working power that proved they were from the Lord?

My Christian friend, do you see any difference in the results of your testimony and that of New Testament saints with the fire from Heaven burning in their bones? You deacons who read this, or other officers of the churches, how does your life and soul-winning witness compare with that of Stephen the martyr, and Philip who evangelized Samaria? There is a holy something, a divine ingredient, a resistless, supernatural Energy—which usually we do not have—that called and led, impassioned and empowered the saints of Bible times! Oh, may He send it upon us! We need the Word of God to burn within our hearts like a fire in our bones, so that we cannot stay.

Most so-called Christian work these days is done in the power of the flesh, not in the power of God. God struck dead Aaron's sons, Nadab and Abihu, because they took strange fire, that is, common fire, not divinely kindled, into the Tabernacle (Lev. 10:1, 2). God struck down Uzzah because he put forth his unanointed hand to steady the ark of God (II Sam. 6:6, 7). King Uzziah, not called of God to be a priest, intruded into that holy work and burned incense in the Temple, and for that he was smitten with leprosy (II Chron. 26:16–21). And the ministry of many a man today is lifeless and dead. The Lord has departed from him, though he, like Samson, may not know it. Too often the Gospel we preach has a barren womb and dry breasts; sons and daughters are not brought forth into the kingdom of God, and the starving saints are not fed! Oh, for fire from Heaven!

The Divine Call

There are not too many preachers; nay, I do not believe there are enough. The Scripture commands, "Let him that heareth say, Come" (Rev. 22:17). And every born-again child of God should, like the converted maniac of Gadara, go home to his friends and his father's house and tell what great things God has done for him. We need, not fewer preachers, for the world is dying and the white harvest is wasting. We should pray the Lord of the harvest to send forth laborers into His harvest. Mothers should give their newborn sons to the ministry, and fathers should bring up their children in the nurture and admonition of the Lord, longing and pleading that God will use them in His own service. There are not too many preachers.

But there are too many preachers preaching without a divine call, a supernatural commission from Heaven. It ought to be said of every preacher, every Sunday school teacher, every soul winner, as it was of John the Baptist, "There was a man sent from God, whose name was _____."

Do you know why the Word of God was in the heart of Jeremiah as a burning in his bones? Read Jeremiah 1:4–9:

"Then the word of the Lord came unto me,

saying, Before I formed thee in the belly I knew thee; and before thou camest forth out of the womb I sanctified thee, and I ordained thee a prophet unto the nations. Then said I, Ah, Lord God! behold, I cannot speak: for I am a child. But the Lord said unto me, Say not, I am a child: for thou shalt go to all that I shall send thee, and whatsoever I command thee thou shalt speak. Be not afraid of their faces: for I am with thee to deliver thee, saith the Lord. Then the Lord put forth his hand, and touched my mouth. And the Lord said unto me, Behold, I have put my words in thy mouth."

Jeremiah was called to preach before he was born! God "sanctified" him, "ordained" him to be a prophet unto the nations. Then in due time the word of the Lord came to him saying he must preach, and God Himself reached down and touched Jeremiah's mouth saying, "I have put my words in thy mouth." God promised detailed instructions, definite leadership, daily preparation. Jeremiah was to go where he was sent, and to speak what was told him, and God promised to deliver His prophet.

If anyone who reads this expects to work for God with blessing, get your Bible down and read again how God called Moses, Isaiah, Elisha and Saul of Tarsus. Read how Jesus called the fishermen to leave their nets, and said, "Follow me, and I will make you fishers of men." Some of you have had this call of God. Some of you know that your ministry was never a matter of human preference. We need to go back again to the starting point and let God put His words in our mouths and hearts and fire in our bones.

Do you remember one spot of holy ground where you

needed to take the shoes off your feet, because God spoke to you from a burning bush? Do you remember the time, like Gideon, when the angel of God spoke to you, and the fleece was first wet, then dry, to prove the call of God? Did you, like Gideon, ask for the "miracles which our fathers told us of" again? and did you receive assurance that the power of God, which was on the prophets of old, would be on you?

Do you remember the time when God lifted you out of sin, put a burning coal to your lips and said, "Lo, this hath touched thy lips; and thine iniquity is taken away, and thy sin purged," as He did to Isaiah when God called him? Did God somewhere strike you down and say to you, as he did to Saul, "I will send thee far hence unto the Gentiles"? Did Jesus ever say to you, as He said to the eleven disciples the day of His resurrection, "As my Father hath sent me, even so send I you"; and did His holy breath blow upon you as He said, "Receive ye the Holy Ghost"? The one hundred twenty tarried ten days in the upper room, until the day of Pentecost was fully come. Have you waited upon God until you received power to be His witness?

O preachers, officers of the churches, Sunday school teachers, soul winners, Christians, we are not fit to serve God until we receive a divine commission, a breath of Heaven, a holy flame! I thank God I know, as definitely as I know I am writing this chapter, that God called me to preach, that He anointed me from my mother's womb to be a soul winner. "To this end was I born." Oh, may I never forget it. I need again that call burned into my soul.

The Soul-Winning Passion
One who would work for Christ must have not only a divine call but a passion that will not let him quit. The fire

you once had will not do for today. One who speaks for Christ must speak as one having authority. He must know that his message is of God. Too many of our sermons are like a supper of leftovers—too long away from the fire! A newsboy cannot sell a paper one day old. God forgive the preacher who expects results from a ministry that has not been touched by the fire of God for weeks or even years!

If a man preaches because he chooses to, he may preach pleasant and lukewarm platitudes to those who come to hear him in a comfortable building and pay him for his trouble; but only the man who preaches because he must, the one with fire in his bones, will preach to men who hate him or deride him or ignore him on the streets, in their homes, in the parks, jails and shops—everywhere.

Paul commanded Timothy, "Preach the word; be instant in season, out of season." For a long time I really wondered at that strange command. Timothy was to preach the Gospel when it was convenient and also when it was not convenient. He was to preach the Gospel when men heard and preach it the same when they would not hear. He was to preach when men supported him and also preach with the same burning passion when he must make tents for bread! The preacher with fire in his bones not only awaits an opportunity; he makes one. He must preach!

This was what Paul meant when he said:

"For though I preach the gospel, I have nothing to glory of: for necessity is laid upon me; yea, woe is unto me, if I preach not the gospel! For if I do this willingly, I have a reward: but if against my will, a dispensation of the gospel is committed unto me." —I Cor. 9:16, 17.

Paul was a bondslave to Jesus Christ, enslaved by the Gospel! He was a debtor both to the Greeks and to the barbarians, both to the wise and to the unwise; for he said, "A dispensation of the gospel is committed unto me." God had placed a holy deposit in Paul's heart that blazed until his dying day, so that he could say, "Woe is unto me, if I preach not the gospel!"

Paul did not mean that God would punish him if he did not preach. I do not think he feared, as some preachers do, that ill health and financial distress would come upon him if he did not preach. Instead, Paul meant, "I am miserable when I can't preach. Life is not worth living if I cannot win souls! I would willingly die to see my brethren, the Jews, saved. I have unceasing sorrow in my heart. I could wish myself accursed from Christ for the sake of lost sinners."

That passion, that compassion, was wrought in the heart of Paul by the Holy Spirit, as it was in the heart of Jeremiah. Without some of that no man or woman is fit to win souls nor able to do much of that holy work.

My beloved readers, this is a divine matter about which I write. We did not save ourselves, call ourselves nor equip ourselves. We need to wait before God until the dross is burned out of our lives, until self-will is dead and the self-life is conformed to the death of Christ, before we can wholly follow the Lord Jesus.

I say frankly that the passion for soul winning, that holy, loving, tearful "MUST" that has burned with consuming flame in the heart of some soul winners, is a supernatural enduement from God. Schools do not give this. Organizations cannot build it. It is supernatural, not natural; divine, not human.

What we need is to tarry before God and so confess and forsake our sins until we are anointed from Heaven. Then the Word of God will be in our hearts like a fire in our bones, as it was with Jeremiah.

O Thou holy God, Thou dying, risen, living Saviour, Thou seeking Spirit, give us this holy passion for sinners, this compelling Gospel, this fire from Heaven!

God's Word in the Preacher's Heart— the Supernatural Message

Jeremiah said, "But his word was in mine heart as a burning fire shut up in my bones." The term, *"his word,"* was supplied by the translators, but that is actually the sense of the Scripture. God had said to Jeremiah, "Behold, I have put my words in thy mouth"; and again and again, many, many times in the book of Jeremiah we are told, "Then the word of the Lord came unto me, saying" (1:4); or, "Moreover the word of the Lord came unto me, saying" (1:11). See also Jeremiah 2:1; 3:6, etc. The words of Jeremiah were literally the words of the Lord.

In Jeremiah 30:2, the Lord commanded Jeremiah, "Write thee all the words that I have spoken unto thee in a book." Jeremiah did, and this proves the verbal inspiration of the Bible. Word-for-word inspiration is God's way of revelation. But it teaches far more than that. When Jeremiah spoke, he spoke the words of the Lord. The message is God's message.

I have heard preachers quote, "My word...shall not return unto me void" (Isa. 55:11), and say that, if a man simply preaches the truth of the Bible, God is certain to bless it. But that is a false interpretation of that Scripture. That verse really means that what God has promised He will bring to pass. It is utterly false to suppose that the Word of the Lord, preached by a cold-hearted, unanointed preacher who preaches in human wisdom and for selfish purposes, will bring its proper fruit, the same as if preached by a man whose heart is set aflame by the Holy Spirit. It takes the power of God to preach the Word of God. The Word of God is not a sword of man but the sword of the Spirit.

All the Bible is God's Word, but it must burn in the preacher's heart. Many cold-hearted Pharisees spent a lifetime studying the Bible, teaching the Bible and trying to follow the Bible; but they were blind leaders of the blind, Jesus said. They compassed land and sea to make a proselyte, then made him twofold more the child of Hell than themselves! The lawyers, Jesus said, experts in the law of Moses, would not enter into the kingdom and yet would not permit others to enter. They had the Word of God, yes, but only the letter of it, not the Spirit. The letter of the law killeth, but the Spirit makes alive. The bare, cold outlines of scriptural facts, as preached by many a preacher, deaden, kill and damn. The Word of God, which comes only through the brain and mouth of a preacher or personal worker, is blighting, fruitless, powerless. In order to be blessed to the hearer, the word of God must be preached from the heart! Jeremiah said, "His word was in mine heart as a burning fire shut up in my bones." A preacher's heart is far more important than his head. It is heart preaching that has power, not head preaching.

In Kansas City during the great Gipsy Smith revival years ago after the service an old preacher came into the room where the Gipsy was sitting. Thousands were being blessed and hundreds saved. The older minister placed his hands upon the evangelist's head and felt about it. "I am trying to find the secret of your success," he said.

"Too high! Too high! My friend, you are too high," Gipsy said. "The secret of whatever success God has given me is not up there but down here," and he placed his hand upon his heart!

I heard this man preach, this gypsy, born in a tent, won by his gypsy father. Gipsy Smith never had a day's schooling from men, yet he preached to the multitudes for sixty years. As he preached, I saw tears course down his cheeks, and my own heart was stirred, warmed and blessed. The Word of God must be in the heart.

Soon after I entered the ministry, I was asked to preach. Somewhat distressed about facing a great Sunday night crowd, I said to a great old minister, Brother G. I. Brittain, "I don't know what to preach tonight." He replied, "And don't you know where to go to find out?" I saw the point, and instead of racking my brain to make a sermon, I went to God in earnest prayer, seeking and begging for a message from Heaven.

This does not belittle the Bible—it adds emphasis to the Bible. Study the Bible? Yes, with all your heart. Preach the Bible? Yes, preach it, all of it; it is God's Word, the infallible, verbally-inspired revelation of God Himself. But preach it with tears, with passion, with fire— preach it from a burning heart set on fire from Heaven!

The apostles were strictly Bible preachers. It is amazing how much Scripture that fisherman Peter used in his sermons recorded in the book of Acts. But mark you; these great preachers, these flaming preachers, these incessant, daily preachers, placed more importance on prayer than on preaching. They asked the multitude to select seven men whom they might appoint over the business of caring for the widows, and "we will give ourselves continually to prayer, and to the ministry of the word" (Acts 6:4).

The Word of God in the brain may lie dormant and unfruitful, but the Word of God in the heart burns like fire in the bones, until one is weary with forbearing and cannot stay! It is the Word of God in the heart, so living, so burning, that one must say, "Woe is unto me, if I preach not the gospel!" Christians need to spend enough time with God that the message of God may really take possession of the heart.

Natural preaching of a supernatural Word will not do. We need a supernatural element in our testimony, a miraculous fire in our ministry. In other words, we need to be filled and transformed by the power of the Holy Spirit so that the message, the power and the fruit are God's.

May God kindle a fire in our bones so that we cannot stay but must tell out God's message!

Praying for Revival

"A prayer of Habakkuk the prophet upon Shigionoth. O Lord, I have heard thy speech, and was afraid: O Lord, revive thy work in the midst of the years, in the midst of the years make known; in wrath remember mercy."—Hab. 3:1, 2.

A revival of Bible religion—how precious and glorious it is! The greatest event that can ever happen on this earth, aside from the return of Christ Himself, is an old-fashioned, Heaven-sent, Holy Spirit revival, when God comes near to the hearts of many men, saving sinners and renewing and rejoicing the hearts of His own people. Revivals are necessary. They are part of God's plan in dealing with His people and with all mankind. Revivals ought to be the chief concern of pastor and people in every church. God calls and prepares evangelists, revivalists. Ephesians 4:11, 12 says:

"And he gave some, apostles; and some, prophets; and some, evangelists; and some, pastors and teachers; For the perfecting of the saints, for the work of the ministry, for the edifying of the body of Christ."

God gives evangelists for the work of edifying the saints, as well as for winning sinners. That proves that God is in favor of revivals.

All of us wish we could stay on the mountaintop. Surely Christians may have blessings day by day. God has provided victory for a Christian all the time. There need be no relapses, no periods of defeat, no fruitlessness. There is abundant power for every Christian. Yet the plain, simple fact is that all God's people need reviving frequently. People do not stay on the mountain of transfiguration, but must return to the valley of suffering.

Revival is a law of nature. Just now

The melancholy days have come,
The saddest of the year,

as the poet says. Green leaves have turned yellow and buff and red and brown. Soon they will all be drab and sear. The sap is gone from the trees. The crops are harvested in the fields. But next spring we will have a revival of leaf and bud and flower and fruit. Seedtime and harvest, sowing and reaping, summer and winter, is the unfailing law of nature. In the millennial reign of Christ we may have eternal summer—the tree of life will bring forth her fruit every month, and the leaves are for the healing of the nations. But as long as Christians have two natures; as long as we live surrounded by manifold temptations; as long as our adversary Satan goes around like a roaring lion seeking whom he may devour (for "we wrestle not against flesh and blood")—that long the saints of God will need periods of refreshing, of revival.

Those who despise revivals ignore the way in which God has dealt with His people. Again and again throughout the

Bible we find accounts of how God sent mighty revivals upon His people—Elijah at Mount Carmel, Daniel in Babylon, Nehemiah in Jerusalem after the captivity, kings Hezekiah and Josiah in Judaea before the captivity; John the Baptist by the river Jordan, Peter and others at Pentecost, Philip in Samaria—all experienced mighty revivals. Bless God for the revivals recorded in the Bible! In fact, the history of God's dealings with the race shows that, when God sent His prophets to warn the people, the inevitable result was either revival or judgment. Today, surely, the only thing that can prevent the terrible wrath of God upon America is a Heaven-sent revival of His blessing and power, a mighty turning to God.

Let no one condemn revivals. You say they do not last? That is not altogether true. Every soul saved in a Heaven-sent revival will shine throughout eternity with a marvelous luster, and all the toil of revivals will be paid for in the coinage of another world. But let us admit that the warmth and the fervor, the new dedication and consecration which we experience in revivals need to be sought again and again. That part of a revival waxes, then wanes, and another revival is needed soon, we frankly admit.

But this does not prove that revivals are a failure; it is simply an argument for the need of another revival, when the first one has waned.

Every traffic *"Safety First"* campaign is temporary. For a time motorists drive more carefully, but soon the inspiration and warning wear off. Has the campaign failed? No, it has saved many lives. The temporariness of the campaign only proves there must be other campaigns.

Plowing is a temporary business. The farmer turns over the soil that in the loosened seedbed seeds may sprout and plants take root. Weeds are turned under. Soon, to be sure, weeds will grow again, and the ground will become packed and hard and will need another plowing. But, meantime, the crop has grown. Food and clothes are made possible by the farmer's plow, even though the work is only temporary. Because the plowing is only temporary is another reason for plowing again.

Revivals, periods of more earnest seeking after God, more frequent and fervent praying, examining our hearts, mortifying the deeds of the flesh, judging our sins—such revivals are in the plan of God for all of us.

Let no church or pastor be satisfied without seeking to have special times of revival. Revivals are not usual, but unusual; not ordinary, but extraordinary. The bane of Christian living and work—the sin which is most certain to befall us—is that our service for Christ may become just a form without the substance—professional, habitual, commonplace and ordinary. The same prayers that once came from the heart now come only from the lips. The Bible reading that was once the fervent seeking after God's truth becomes merely a dutiful habit. Then there is need for a revival.

"O Lord, I Have Heard Thy Speech, and Was Afraid"

Habakkuk lived in a time of terrible declension and worldliness. It was just before the captivity of Judah. The prophecy begins with this title, "The burden which Habakkuk the prophet did see." "Burden" means a message of weight and sorrow, a promised punishment. The second to fourth verses of the first chapter of the prophecy say,

"O Lord, how long shall I cry, and thou wilt not

*hear! even cry out unto thee of violence, and thou
wilt not save! Why dost thou shew me iniquity,
and cause me to behold grievance? for spoiling
and violence are before me: and there are that
raise up strife and contention. Therefore the law is
slacked, and judgment doth never go forth: for the
wicked doth compass about the righteous; therefore wrong judgment proceedeth."*

Habakkuk, amazed and grieved at the sin, violence
and idolatry about him, cries out to God for judgment and
punishment on the people. Then in chapter 2, the answer
of God is given. Verses 6, 9, 12, 15 and 19 promise separate and terrible woes upon Israel. Then in our text in
chapter 3, Habakkuk cries out, "O Lord, I have heard thy
speech, and was afraid: O Lord, revive thy work in the
midst of the years, in the midst of the years make known;
in wrath remember mercy."

A TIME OF WICKEDNESS, WORLDLINESS, BLOOD-
SHED AND THE WRATH OF GOD IS A GOOD TIME
FOR REVIVAL! In fact, such times cry out for revival. The
more a revival is needed, the more willing God is to give it.
The more a revival is needed, the more will some people
realize the need. Christians will be led more earnestly to
pray. Some sinners will be more willing to listen. The
preacher's sharp message against sin will be more
emphatic, more startling, yet more quickly believed by
some who have found that the way of the transgressor is
hard and have seen the fruits of sin.

When Habakkuk heard the woes which God pro-
nounced upon His people, the warning of God frightened
him and led to earnest prayer for revival.

Let preachers consider and take notice! Revivals, old-fashioned, Heaven-sent revivals, are ordinarily preceded by plain, sharp, dogmatic, positive preaching. The preacher who faithfully, fearlessly and with a holy abandon condemns sin in high places and in low, among the saints of God and in the wicked world about him, will cause conviction on the part of sinners, and a keen hunger and thirst for revival on the part of God's people. Penitent seeking after God follows faithful proclamation of the divine warning. Nineveh repented only after Jonah preached, "Yet forty days, and Nineveh shall be overthrown." The marvelous revival under John the Baptist came from such preaching as this:

> *"And now also the axe is laid unto the root of the trees: therefore every tree which bringeth not forth good fruit is hewn down, and cast into the fire. I indeed baptize you with water unto repentance: but he that cometh after me is mightier than I, whose shoes I am not worthy to bear: he shall baptize you with the Holy Ghost, and with fire: Whose fan is in his hand, and he will throughly purge his floor, and gather his wheat into the garner; but he will burn up the chaff with unquenchable fire."*—Matt. 3:10–12.

That was a plain warning of the wrath of God against sin, that the Jewish religious leaders, yea, even the nation itself would be cut down like a fruitless tree if it did not repent and get right with God. More than that, there was a plain warning of the fires of Hell—that Jesus will "burn up the chaff with unquenchable fire."

The great revival under Hezekiah was preceded by

such plain preaching as this in II Chronicles 29:6–9:

> *"For our fathers have trespassed, and done that which was evil in the eyes of the Lord our God, and have forsaken him, and have turned away their faces from the habitation of the Lord, and turned their backs. Also they have shut up the doors of the porch, and put out the lamps, and have not burned incense nor offered burnt-offerings in the holy place unto the God of Israel.*
>
> *"Wherefore the wrath of the Lord was upon Judah and Jerusalem, and he hath delivered them to trouble, to astonishment, and to hissing, as ye see with your eyes. For, lo, our fathers have fallen by the sword, and our sons and our daughters and our wives are in captivity for this."*

Other Old Testament revivals were preceded by the reading of the law, with solemn judgments promised upon those who should depart from God.

Let preachers then take heart. In the time of war, the time of sin and worldliness, of unbelief and modernism, of gambling and drunkenness and adultery—that is the time for revivals, provided the prophets of God will be true in declaring God's wrath on sin. If preachers will be true to God, then people will cry out, "O Lord, I have heard thy speech, and was afraid," and will beg God for a revival.

"O Lord, Revive Thy Work"

My brother, the work is the Lord's. We have a right to expect Him to repair it, to renew it, to bless it.

First of all, what happened to me was of God. When I was an undone sinner, it was God who loved me and prepared salvation for me at the fearful price of the death of Jesus on the cross. It was the Holy Spirit who sought me, who ran me down, who knocked so insistently and pleaded so tenderly that I surrendered and was saved. It was the blood of Christ that paid my debt and cleansed me from all sin. My salvation is all of grace. "Not by works of righteousness which we have done, but according to his mercy he saved us." If my heart is not as warm as it ought to be, if my service is not pleasing and acceptable to God, then nothing is more reasonable than that I should come to God for His remedy.

I do not blame God for my faults. He is not responsible for my sins. My failures are not His failures. Yet, in some sense, I am not my own. The problems of my Christian life are not my problems after all, but His. I am bought with the blood of Christ. The work is Christ's. I am "his workmanship".

When buying a new car, you receive a warranty for ninety days. During that time any defective part must be replaced free of charge. If some adjustment was not properly made or if there was some fault in the manufacture of the automobile, you may drive back to the dealer and have the matter attended to at his charge.

But how much better is the guarantee that God gives a sinner when He saves him! The Lord not only took care of the first cost, but all the upkeep on your salvation! It is everlasting life that He promised, and even the more abundant life! Troubled, backslidden reader, the work you need done is God's work. You have a perfect right to lift up your poor, feeble hands to Him and cry out, "O Lord, revive *Thy* work. I am Yours. I need a blessing. I need spiritual food and drink. I need new cleansing, new love, new joy, new power! Father, I am Your child. I have nowhere else to go. Lord, *revive Thy work.*"

As conversion is a divine business, so is the call to preach. There is a romance about preaching the Gospel. There is a heavenly fragrance about telling sinners that the risen, glorified Christ died for them, and teaching the people of God what their calling and inheritance are.

But preachers do not stay on fire for God. We sometimes find that the Gospel is not as sweet to our own ears as it once was. We may serve others at God's table yet ourselves go hungry. Preachers need revivals. But we have a right to go to the Lord and say, "O Lord, revive thy work in the midst of the years." We who have been called to preach have a right to a fresh vision, a fresh anointing, a fresh commission.

Many great business firms feel personally responsible for their salesmen. And every so often a salesman is taken to "the home office" or to "the factory" for fresh inspiration and reward.

When an automobile manufacturer puts out a new model, special sessions are held for automobile dealers and salesmen. They are given the facts about the new model. They are given the best sales talk. They see with their own eyes the beauties of the lovely machine. They test for themselves its wonderful performance. They return to sell it with enthusiasm and inspiration. The automobile manufacturer knows that he is responsible for his dealers.

So, my brother preacher, we have a right to go to God and ask Him for new help, just like Elijah fleeing from Jezebel, or like John the Baptist languishing in prison.

We are His workmanship. May God revive His own work in the hearts of His preachers!

"...In the Midst of the Years, in the Midst of the Years Make Known"

Years ago at many a baptizing by a riverbank they sang the old song:

> **Oh, how happy are they**
> **Who the Saviour obey,**
> **   And whose treasures are laid up above;**
> **Tongue can never express**
> **The sweet peace, joy and rest**
> **   Of a soul in its earliest love.**

Even the Scripture speaks of the first love. The church at Ephesus is warned of God, "I have somewhat against thee, because thou hast left thy first love" (Rev. 2:4).

Do you remember the sweetness, the fresh ecstasy when you first trusted Christ? Do you remember how you loved Christians, how you longed to see sinners saved? Do you remember with what fervor you prayed, and how rich were those passages in the Bible with which you first became familiar after you were saved?

Oh, that God would give us again the freshness of our beginnings! Preacher, do you remember your first sermons, your first revivals? How sweet is the first love!

It is "in the midst of the years" that we need revivals. A watch, when first wound, may keep accurate time; but if it goes too long without winding, it begins slowly to lose time. A preacher who goes too long without winding does not have the power he once had! Christians need rewinding, i.e., reviving "in the midst of the years."

Tendency to Backslide

It is a strange thing, this tendency to backslide after one has long been settled in the Christian life. I have seen many a young Christian give up cigarettes or picture shows or gambling, and do it gladly, do it easily, to begin the soul-winning life. But little by little, later on, the older habits laid aside have a tendency to reappear "in the midst of the years." I have found that the drunkard, wonderfully saved, often leaves his old companions, gives a fervent testimony wherever he goes, and experiences all the power and victory of a Christian life for weeks or months or sometimes years; and then, when he ceases to be afraid of the old habit, when he is off his guard, when he has settled down into a more or less routine service, he may slip into the old sins again.

Christian, look out for the settled period "in the midst of the years." Then is when we should pray earnestly for a revival. Then is our time of danger.

Many a man marries a lovely girl and lives with her happily through the strenuous early years of married life. He must work hard in business. He loves his wife. There is the holy thrill of new babies and the responsibilities of fatherhood.

But after awhile, "in the midst of the years," when a man is well established in business, when his home seems safe and his children are maturing satisfactorily, many a man falls prey to the siren voice of an evil woman.

How many homes are broken after the children are grown! How many a man takes up gambling or crooked business after he has made a success in life! Those middle years, those settled years, are times of great need for revival.

I believe that a nation is in great danger after it has passed the first stages, when the government is settled, when its frontiers are developed, when prosperity and independence are safely assured, when danger seems a thing of the past. Then there comes the slow decay of manhood, corruption in politics, worldliness in the church, atheism in the school and license in the home. When America was young, we believed in God. Our greatest danger has come "in the midst of the years." Oh, the need for revival in the midst of the years!

"In Wrath Remember Mercy"

God had expressed His wrath on the sins of Judah. Captivity and woe were promised. There is every evidence that the wrath of God is on the world today. A view of the world shows a dark picture. Murderous communism has overrun much of Europe. The nuclear bomb and other war techniques threaten to destroy the entire civilization. We are in days of wrath!

Government of the people, by the people and for the people is disappearing from the earth. Drugs and drunkenness are increasing as are crimes of every kind, and accidents. Even nature shows the wrath of God upon His wicked creatures; drought, flood and pestilence add to the terrors of unemployment. We are in days of wrath! Preachers ought to preach this fearlessly.

I expect judgment to fall upon America. Communism rears its defiant head, seeking to bring anarchy and atheism to our land, to overthrow our government and close our churches. I say, these are days of wrath, and every preacher should be a warning prophet.

But, thank God, days of wrath can be days of mercy,

too! Let every Christian pray, "O Lord, revive thy work in the midst of the years, in the midst of the years make known; in wrath remember mercy." Troublous, sinful days are just the days to pray for revival.

I have found that peoples' hearts are terribly hard in these wicked days. Many men will not hear the Gospel. Many women will laugh in a preacher's face. Many youths scoff at religion and Heaven and God. But I find that, where the chastening hand of God has fallen, there oftentimes men listen to the Gospel! When I preach a funeral sermon, I preach revival, and you may be sure that there are broken hearts who will hear it. Days of wrath and judgment are also days of mercy. When God stretches out His hand, He does it in mercy as well as in wrath. We should expect sinners to turn to God as a result of every great calamity.

In Wichita Falls, Texas, some years ago, I came upon an awful scene one night, just after a car had turned over with four young people. The car was ruined. One young woman was so badly injured that she spent months in the hospital; though, that night we did not know how seriously she was hurt. I took them in my car to their homes at midnight. When I suggested that we have a time of prayer and thank God that I was not bringing home to the mother a dead girl, they were eager to pray. They knew it was a warning from God. Two of that number were happily converted, and the other two— backslidden Christians—made confession of their waywardness and promised to attend services the following Sunday, to line up with God's people and serve Him. They knew that it was a time of wrath, and they sought mercy.

My dear reader, the time of judgment is a time to call on God for a revival.

In the jails, I have seen hundreds claim Christ as their Saviour. There are several reasons why I liked to preach to people in jail. One reason is, they needed it. Another reason is that they couldn't get away. But the best reason is that they wanted the Gospel. A man who is sentenced to several years in the penitentiary listens very respectfully when you preach that the way of the transgressor is hard; and in many, many cases he rejoices to know that his sins, though scarlet, can be made as white as snow. Take heart, my friends. I believe that we are in days of wrath, but I know that we have a right to pray that God will send a mighty revival in such a day as this.

The great Dwight L. Moody never tired of telling how God blessed and saved souls as he went among the wounded soldiers of the Union Army, following the great battles of the Civil War. They were ripe for the Gospel.

The clouds are heavy on every side. Christians must be grieved and heavyhearted, if they feel that they are their brothers' keepers, and if they have loved ones unsaved. Then let us pray, like Habakkuk, that God will revive His work in the midst of these evil years, and that in these days of wrath He will remember mercy.

"A Prayer of Habakkuk"
How shall we have a revival? Dear reader, let us pray! Habakkuk prayed for a revival. At Pentecost, the apostles and others waited and prayed for a revival. In Nineveh, they fasted and prayed day and night, so that neither man nor beast ate nor drank. They put on sackcloth and ashes and ceased every man from his violence. And God heard

from Heaven and repented of that which He had planned to do and did it not.

Let it be settled once for all that revivals are divine manifestations. A revival is a miracle of God, not natural, but supernatural; not ordinary, but extraordinary; not human, but divine. Only God can give a revival.

Elijah well said to the men on Mount Carmel about the sacrifice, "Put no fire under." God must put the fire on the altar if we are really to have a revival. Elijah could repair the altar that was torn down; he could lay the wood in order; he could slay the bullock and dress it, but only God could give the revival fire!

Before Pentecost the apostles had been breathed upon; and when Christ was glorified, according to promise, they received the Holy Ghost to live in their bodies (John 7:37-39; 20:22). Jesus had opened their understanding that they might understand the Scriptures and had taught them in all the Scriptures the things concerning Himself (Luke 24:27, 44, 45). They had received their Great Commission, but even then the revival did not come until with all their hearts and with one accord they continued in prayer and supplication (Acts 1:14).

An old, old song that I used to hear when a boy in country churches impressed me greatly:

> **Brethren, we have met to worship,**
> **And adore the Lord our God;**
> **Will you pray with all your power,**
> **While we try to preach the Word?**
>
> **All is vain unless the Spirit**
> **Of the Holy One come down;**
> **Brethren, pray, and holy manna**
> **Will be showered all around.**
>
> **Brethren, see poor sinners round you,**

> **Trembling on the brink of woe;**
> **Death is coming, Hell is moving—**
> **Can you bear to see them go?**
>
> **See our fathers and our mothers**
> **And our children sinking down;**
> **Brethren, pray, and holy manna**
> **Will be showered all around!**

That may be old-fashioned, but according to the Word of God, it is true. Habakkuk prayed! It is PRAYER to Almighty God that brings revivals!

In these modern days, people think much of a trained ministry. We are strong on organization and on equipment. There is a subtle change going on in our thinking, and we begin to persuade ourselves that mass revivals are over, that God does not work miracles any longer, that what preachers need is more culture, not more Christ. Psychology seems more important than power, and organizing is a good deal easier than agonizing! "The supper room" is more popular than "the upper room" in the modern church. But after all, there is only One who can bring us out of our difficulties in our nation, in our homes, and in our churches, yea, in the depths of our own hearts. We need a revival! Only God can give it. Then I beg you who read this, let us pray!

If a lost sinner is reading this who is undone, away from God, and has never found peace, then I remind you that you have a right to pray for salvation. Romans 10:13 says, "For whosoever shall call upon the name of the Lord shall be saved." If you want forgiveness, salvation and peace, you can have it today wherever you are, if you will ask God for it. The publican in the Temple prayed, "God be merciful to me a sinner," and went down to his house justified (Luke 18:13,14). The thief on the cross cried out to Jesus, "Lord, remember me when thou comest into thy kingdom," and Jesus forgave him and said, "To day shalt thou be with me in paradise" (Luke 23:42, 43).

It is God who forgives sinners. It is God who changes the heart. God will save you today, right now, if you will trust Him. Jesus said, "Him that cometh to me I will in no wise cast out" (John 6:37).

You can have a revival of your own just now as you sit in your chair, if you will call on the God of revivals. Christians everywhere can have revivals, if earnestly, persistently, with holy abandon, with heart-searching confession and humility and surrender, they pray, as did Habakkuk:

"O Lord, I have heard thy speech, and was afraid: O Lord, revive thy work in the midst of the years, in the midst of the years make known; in wrath remember mercy."—Hab. 3:2.

Evangelistic Preaching

"I charge thee therefore before God, and the Lord Jesus Christ, who shall judge the quick and the dead at his appearing and his kingdom; Preach the word; be instant in season, out of season; reprove, rebuke, exhort with all longsuffering and doctrine. For the time will come when they will not endure sound doctrine; but after their own lusts shall they heap to themselves teachers, having itching ears; And they shall turn away their ears from the truth, and shall be turned unto fables. But watch thou in all things, endure afflictions, do the work of an evangelist, make full proof of thy ministry."—II Tim. 4:1–5.

"Do the work of an evangelist." This message is given to a pastor. Paul said, "I besought thee to abide still at Ephesus, when I went into Macedonia, that thou mightest charge some that they teach no other doctrine" (I Tim. 1:3). Timothy was evidently a pastor, still Paul says to him, "Do the work of an evangelist." "Preach the word; be instant in season, out of season; reprove, rebuke, exhort with all longsuffering and doctrine."

Most of our finest soul winners have been pastors. We think sometimes that the evangelist is the man to win souls, and the pastor is merely to feed the sheep; but there is nothing like that in God's program and plan. When God sets men on fire to win souls, they often, yea, generally, have been pastors. For instance, Charles Spurgeon was never known as an evangelist, yet the tens of thousand he won to Christ prove that he did the work of an evangelist, though his entire ministry was given as a pastor.

Many people think of R. A. Torrey as an evangelist, but for years he was pastor of the Chicago Avenue Church, which eventually became the great Moody Memorial Church. His was pastoral preaching.

Charles G. Finney was a pastor for several years in New York City and elsewhere. The great soul winners have been pastors—Talmage and Len Broughton and George W. Truett and H. A. Ironside, and many others whose names I could mention.

To please God, a pastor must do evangelistic preaching. And I make bold to say that any man whom God calls, whatever gifts God may have given him should be used for winning souls. The Saviour said, "Follow me, and I will make you fishers of men." Whenever God calls a man to follow Him, He means to make him a soul winner.

I know preachers who have said, "Well, I am going to settle down and become a teaching pastor." Such a pastor is a backslider, "at ease in Zion," lukewarm, not willing to pay the sacrificial price to be a real soul winner—blood, sweat, tears, separation, consecration, purging, and day by day denying self (Luke 9:23), going "outside the gate," bearing the reproach of Christ.

Though now in full-time evangelistic work, it was only in 1940 that I closed a pastorate of nearly eight years. In those years, some 7,000 or 8,000 people made professions of faith under the ministry of that church and pastor. Now I say, not to take any credit, that God intends the head of a local congregation, an overseer and pastor and bishop, to be a soul winner, and to train and send out soul winners.

Evangelistic Preaching Must Boldly Attack Sin

Now what kind of preaching is evangelistic? I suggest, first, that pastors must preach against sin if they are to have many saved.

The other day in a service my dear wife talked to a woman about her soul who had no conception about the plan of salvation. My wife said later, "I didn't know where to begin with her." I said, "You must remember, when dealing with a sinner, you begin with the fact of sin."

A man may say, "I don't believe as you do. I am not a member of your church." Never mind; the one common ground on which to approach every sinner is the fact of sin. That is where God begins, and that is where God wants preachers to begin. Preachers ought to condemn sin.

A certain preacher said about my preaching, "That man knows nothing about grace." I know about grace, but one way I know about grace is that I know what an awful, Hell-bound, Hell-deserving sinner I was and am. I know how God saved me from the torments of the damned. There is no grace unless there is first sin. No use preaching grace unless first men know they are wicked, Hell-bound sinners. Only the grace of God can save, but grace saves only convicted, confessed sinners.

We need to preach against sin; Bible preachers did.

Elijah hated sin. When he prayed down fire from Heaven, he took the prophets of Baal down to the brook and slew them himself. Elijah was known everywhere as a hard preacher. He told Ahab that God would destroy every man of his whole family, and the kingdom would be changed. Elijah was known as God's man, preaching against sin.

There is Jeremiah. We learn in the book of Jeremiah that he said, "I cannot speak: for I am a child." But God told him He would give him a face of brass against the people. 'Do not fear their faces nor their words; but preach. Whether they hear or whether they forbear, preach what I give you. I will put My words in your mouth, and they will know a prophet of God has been among them.' Oh, may God give us men like Jeremiah, who was called to preach plainly against sin!

New Testament preachers preached the same way. By the river of Jordan John the Baptist preached, "Repent." Some people think that is out of date. They talk very wisely about the "baptism of John," as if that were Old Testament, as if that were law. Don't you believe it! That was the only baptism Jesus had. That was the only baptism that Peter had, and James and John and the rest of the apostles, and all the New Testament Christians of that day.

John the Baptist preached New Testament sermons. He preached grace, he preached the Gospel, but he preached first that men are awful sinners and must repent! He preached, "The axe is laid unto the root of the trees." And when some came to be baptized who didn't show any evidence of a changed heart toward sin and toward God, John the Baptist rebuked them, saying, "O generation of vipers, who hath warned you to flee from the wrath to come? Bring forth therefore fruits meet for repentance" (Matt. 3:7, 8).

Preachers today don't like to look into the faces of the people in the pews and declare, "You bunch of snakes, you generation of vipers, who has warned you to flee from the wrath to come?" But John the Baptist did. He was sometimes personal in it. He came face to face with King Herod and said, 'It isn't right for you to have your brother's wife. It is shameful, adulterous.' It cost him his freedom, and he was put in prison, and eventually it cost him his head; but he was a preacher without fear or favor, and he was honored of God. Jesus said that never was one born of woman who was greater than John the Baptist.

Now to be evangelistic in our preaching, we must first preach against sin. Bible preachers won souls because they preached against sin.

Jesus also denounced sin. If you want to know how Jesus preached, read Matthew 23. Seven times He calls the scribes and Pharisees hypocrites. "Woe unto you, scribes and Pharisees, hypocrites." He calls them "whited sepulchres." He calls them "blind leaders of the blind." He says they are "wolves in sheep's clothing." He says, "Fill ye up then the measure of your fathers. Ye serpents, ye generation of vipers, how can ye escape the damnation of hell?"

That is how Jesus preached. He took a rope, tied knots in it, made a good whip, then drove out of the Temple the worldly and covetous moneychangers. He called it a "den of thieves"! He not only scattered the beasts of burden, the doves and the sheep that people sold, but He turned over their tables! He didn't say politely, "Will you please take the tables and step outside?"

Can't you see those covetous old Pharisees chasing the coins that rolled over the marble floor, when Jesus kicked the tables over and cracked that whip and drove the people out? I say, Jesus preached plainly against sin. You can't have people saved unless first you bring a consciousness of sin and preach the wrath of God on sin and call for repentance from sin.

That dear woman at the well of Sychar in Samaria was won because Jesus showed her she was a sinner. Jesus was ever so tender, ever so kind, but when she found the Saviour and went to tell the people about it, the thing that stuck in her mind, the thing that broke her heart and transformed her life was that Jesus knew all about her sin! She went back and told the men, "Come, see a man, which told me all things that ever I did" (John 4:29). Jesus didn't really say to her, "You are an adulterous harlot; you have already lived with five different men, and are living with one now who is not your husband," but He made her say it. He put His finger on the hellish sin in her life.

Nobody is going to have conviction settle on congregations where he preaches and have hardened sinners, bootleggers, fallen women, convicts and dope fiends saved, without preaching on sin. No preacher will reach these proud and haughty evolutionists and atheists unless he preaches against sin.

Sin is the point of contact between the preacher and the sinner. It is God's point of contact, too. You must do something about sin. You must repent, turn away from sin. That is how Jesus preached.

Peter stood and preached at Pentecost to the crowd that crucified the Saviour, perhaps looking straight into the eyes of the soldier who put the spear in His side. He was certainly looking into the eyes of the priests, Pharisees and leaders of the synagogue who had mocked Him while He died. He afterwards said to them, 'You killed the Prince of life and desired a murderer to be granted unto you. You have crucified and slain the Lord of glory, but God has raised Him up, whereof we are witnesses.' When later they called Peter and John to account; saying, "Ye have filled Jerusalem with your doctrine," they said, "We ought to obey God rather than men." God, give us more Peters and Johns who will preach boldly to the Pharisees of this day! We need preaching against sin.

Stephen stood and preached, "Ye stiffnecked and uncircumcised in heart and ears, ye do always resist the Holy Ghost: as your fathers did, so do ye." It cost Stephen his life; but He was filled with the Spirit of God, and he preached against sin. Such preaching by Stephen, I have no doubt, convicted the young man Saul so that he never got away from Stephen's dying testimony and his piercing words, until he met Jesus on the road to Damascus and became Paul the apostle! What if Stephen had failed that day! He preached sharp against sin. His hearers became so angry that they literally "gnashed on him with their teeth" (Acts 7:54).

How boldly Paul preached against sin! Paul stood before Felix; "and as he reasoned of righteousness, temperance, and judgment to come, Felix trembled" (Acts 24:25). If we preached more on judgment, temperance and righteousness these days, we, too, could cause sinners to tremble as Paul did!

Paul, you say, was a preacher of grace? He was also a preacher of "righteousness, temperance, and judgment."

The people trembled, even the rulers. Though Paul had chains dangling from his handcuffs and anklets, yet they trembled when he preached against sin in the power of the Holy Spirit.

How flaming, how personal, how insulting was Paul's preaching sometimes! Standing in the court of Sergius Paulus, Paul faced Elymas the sorcerer and announced, "O full of all subtilty and all mischief, thou child of the devil, thou enemy of all righteousness, wilt thou not cease to pervert the right ways of the Lord?" (Acts 13:10). And in answer to such boldness and faith, God struck the vile sinner blind, and the deputy was wonderfully saved.

If you do not go for that type preaching, then remember that it followed days of fasting and prayer, when Paul and Barnabas, "being sent forth by the Holy Ghost, departed" on this missionary journey. Spirit-filled preachers must hate sin and say so. God will back up such men with wonders and signs and with great conversions, as He did then.

What kind of subjects shall a man preach on in evangelistic preaching? Preach on booze! Paul preached on "temperance" (Acts 24:25). There is plenty in the Bible like, "Wine is a mocker, strong drink is raging: and whosoever is deceived thereby is not wise" (Prov. 20:1). Some people say, "I don't believe in a preacher's getting into politics." Politics or no politics, an honest pastor must denounce the horrible sin of the liquor traffic, if he is to see God move wonderfully in saving drunkards.

One dear woman said, "O Brother Rice, we have the dearest preacher. He doesn't meddle in either politics or religion!" What she meant was that he never expressed himself on any civic question where there was a difference of opinion and never got on any question of doctrine where there was a difference of opinion.

No preacher can please God who stays out of controversy. God has a controversy with sin. It is sin that nailed Jesus to the cross. It is sin that is populating Hell. It is sin that fills every graveyard, every hospital, every jail. It is sin that blights every home that is broken by divorce. It is sin that a preacher must hate, denounce, expose! God hates sin; and if a preacher doesn't hate it, people will not repent of sin. Preach on booze! Preach on the scarlet sin, adultery. Some cheeks will turn red with shame, and some won't like it; but it will bring repentance.

Preach on the dance. Tell people that it is rotten with sin. Tell them they dance because they enjoy the lust, the deliberate inflaming of passion! Yes, preach on the dance.

Preach on the movies. Tell people what they are and what they will do; that they are made by vile, lewd people, holding up rotten moral standards, breaking down respect for marriage, pure love, hard work, God and the Bible. Denounce the lust, the crime, the bawdy vulgarity of the movies.

Preach against the lodges. Tell people that God commands Christians: "Come out from among them, and be ye separate."

Preach against evolution and false cults. Preach on death, sin, Hell, judgment! Such preaching with boldness, with love, with tears, with Scripture, and with faith will bring great revivals and will save hardened sinners.

Some preacher says, "I like to preach on John 3:16—'God so loved the world.'" That is fine. But here is another verse from the Bible: "For our God is a consuming fire." Why not preach that, too? Or, "It is a fearful thing to fall into the hands of the living God" is also in the Bible. So is, "For the wages of sin is death." Here is another one in the Bible: "Be sure your sin will find you out." Here is another one in the Bible: "Be not deceived; God is not mocked: for whatsoever a man soweth, that shall he also reap."

May God give us grace to preach against sin!

Somebody says, "An evangelist can do that, but a pastor cannot." But I would remind you again that for these years as a pastor, I have preached the same, using the same texts and the same kind of language—plain, sharp and clear. Others say, "You will make somebody mad." Of course you will. "They will quit giving money." Of course they will. But is that your goal in preaching? "Somebody will leave the church." Certainly they will; maybe even you will have to leave. Sure! John the Baptist lost his head. Stephen was stoned to death. Paul was put in prison. Jesus Christ was crucified.

God have pity on a preacher who is not willing to suffer for real convictions. May God put *men* in the pulpit these days, not sissies!

The pulpit has lost the confidence and respect of the world these days. We have soft-spoken preachers who never hurt anybody's feelings, never offend anybody, never cross anybody, never awaken anybody, never arouse anybody, *and rarely save anybody!*

Allow me to give you a personal reference. Last fall a wicked woman came to hear me preach. She had cursed God and said she would never serve Him because her mother had died. As she talked about it later, she said, "Oh, that preacher!"—with hate in her voice as she said it—"I have lost nine pounds going to hear him preach! I don't know why I come back."

Our preaching should make people sleepless at night, cause them to lie awake, stare into the dark, afraid to go to sleep. It should be preaching that makes people go to their closets in prayer. We need to break up the ground before we sow the seed. God give us preachers like that. These sissy-britches, peace-at-any price preachers; these "good-Lord and good-Devil," milk-and-cider preachers will never bring a revival. All the world is under judgment and the wrath of God.

My dear preacher-brethren—God bless you! My preacher-brethren, reprove and rebuke, as well as exhort. Preach Bible doctrine!

Evangelistic Preaching Must Be of Red-Hot Earnestness

What else about this preaching? If you want the Lord's power and blessing on you in saving souls, you must mean business. Evangelistic preaching must have a certain fervor of heart that involves tears in preparation and perhaps in delivery; that involves a straightforwardness, a zeal which makes it so that when he preaches an evangelistic message he may speak so fast that he will mispronounce the words and sometimes lose the trend of his well-prepared discourse. He may not say what he had planned, but he is led by the Holy Ghost. He may appear awkward and what he says may be more or less abrupt and uncouth.

God, give us back the fervor, the tears, the boldness of men of God of other days! We must have a mean-business attitude about our preaching that will make it colorful, informal and unorthodox as to the method, though orthodox always as to God's message.

Why shouldn't a preacher stand or sit, cry or laugh or sing while he preaches? People on the stage do it. Why can't a man laugh and weep for joy over Heaven? Why can't he blaze against sin? Why not an informal sincerity to get results? Why must a preacher have a sonorous voice, a stilted attitude, a pious smirk and platitudinous commonplaceness in the pulpit?

God, give us men who mean business in the pulpit! I did when I played college football. I did when I was out in business. Then why shouldn't I mean business as a preacher of the Gospel?

That means that our preaching will sometimes have to be sensational. If we preach as we ought about sin, death, judgment, the second coming, and the wrath of God, we will sometimes be called sensational. The people said about Paul and Barnabas, "These that have turned the world upside down are come hither also." Remember, Peter and John were dragged before the Sanhedrin, and the priests said, "Ye have filled Jerusalem with your doctrine." When there is a riot and a preacher now and then gets put in jail and someone spits in his face or throws rotten eggs and tomatoes; when drunkards, harlots, convicts and dopeheads are saved, then you are going to have a sensation. Don't avoid it, but pray God to arouse and alarm people.

I don't mean trick and fake sensational stunts. I mean the boldness of God, the fire of the Spirit, the kind of preaching that brings men to their knees, with tears of repentance, trusting in Jesus Christ, or which sends them out in hate, gnashing their teeth, as they did with Christ and Stephen.

Depend on the Miracle-Working Word of God

O my fellow preachers, believe the Word and press it hot on people's hearts. "He that goeth forth and weepeth, bearing precious seed, shall doubtless come again with rejoicing, bringing his sheaves with him" (Ps. 126:6). Take the Word of God. Plant it, believe it, expect God to bless it. Depend on the Word of God. Memorize a lot of it. When you come to preach, claim the promises. Then when you give an invitation, give the actual words of the Scripture to cling to, and get men to meet God on His promises. It isn't hard to be saved. The reason people are not saved is that in their wicked hearts they are not willing to turn from sin and take God at His Word. Use the Word. It is "quick, and powerful, and sharper than any twoedged sword" (Heb. 4:12). "Is not my word like as a fire saith the Lord; and like a hammer that breaketh the rock in pieces?" (Jer. 23:29).

Pull for Results Always

We must mean business, and that means we will pull for results. O my brothers, let us so preach so that if an unsaved person is present we will seek to win him while we can. And if you preach to a crowd and there are no unconverted present, then urge the Christians to do all they can in winning souls. You can't preach to the sinners if they are not there, but you can preach to the people who will reach sinners and bring them in. Let's set people on fire for winning souls. Let's pull for results.

I preached many funerals, especially when I was pastor and had a daily radio service. I made God a promise: I would never preach a funeral service without making plain the plan of salvation and urging men to repent. I have given an invitation at many, many funerals and had people saved.

As a young woman came down the stairs from a dance hall on the second floor at Magnolia and Hemphill Streets in Fort Worth, Texas, her husband met her and jealously stabbed her to death. I was called to preach the funeral. That nightclub crowd, that underworld crowd, that wild and profligate crowd, that wayward-daughter and prodigal-son crowd, packed the funeral parlor. I preached the plan of salvation. As I called for sinners, eight came down to claim Christ as Saviour.

"But people will be offended," a preacher says. Then announce ahead of time that that is the only kind of sermon you will preach. I promised God I wouldn't preach one kind of Gospel in a revival meeting and another kind at a funeral. I will never preach into Heaven some old profligate, ungodly wretch who would not repent while he had an opportunity.

Get people saved when you marry a couple. Get people saved at funerals. Get people saved in Sunday school classes. Get people saved in the morning as well as in the evening service. Get people saved at Rotary clubs, at Kiwanis luncheons. Anyplace a preacher has a right to speak, he has a right to talk about salvation.

Dr. L. R. Scarborough had a way of saying, "Any end of the Gospel is good, just so it is the hot end." Deliver the Gospel hot and win souls!

A Definite Enduement of Holy Spirit Power Essential to Soul-Winning Preaching

Another word about evangelistic preaching is this: It must be preaching with a definite enduement of Holy Spirit power. Magnetism won't do it; personality never saved a soul; psychology never won a sinner.

I read an article the other day by a man who was lamenting that in these days we can't have revivals, that there is a great falling away. He said: "We had so many preachers; we had chalk talks, motion pictures, special music—all those—yet we didn't get but about fifty people saved."

They didn't have a musical saw at Pentecost, but three thousand people were saved: John the Baptist didn't win them by wearing a cowboy suit and bringing a long lariat into the pulpit. Elijah didn't set out to Mount Carmel with a boy prodigy who could play an accordion. It takes more than these incidentals, more than cowbells and tricks and solos. *It takes the fire of Almighty God!* Nobody is going to win souls and have a revival, unless he has an anointing from God.

When Jesus came to be baptized and waited and prayed, the Holy Ghost came on Him like a dove, and Jesus was anointed. Then He went back to the synagogue in Nazareth and read Isaiah 61:1:

> *"The Spirit of the Lord God is upon me; because the Lord hath anointed me to preach good tidings unto the meek; he hath sent me to bind up the brokenhearted, to proclaim liberty to the captives, and the opening of the prison to them that are bound."*

Jesus never worked a miracle nor preached a sermon nor won a soul *until He was anointed!* Perfect and sinless and holy He was, but He began His ministry after He was anointed to preach.

Sometimes preachers preach so dully and lifelessly that people say, "I am afraid he has not been called to preach." That isn't the answer. He has been *called* but not *anointed*. He has been called, but he hasn't answered, hasn't been fitted.

Let us learn a lesson from Peter, James, John and the other apostles. Before Pentecost they were saved and had been given the Great Commission. Christ had opened their hearts to understand the Scriptures. They were filled with joy at the appearance of the resurrected Saviour. "Then were the disciples glad, when they saw the Lord" (John 20:20). Jesus had breathed on them and said, "Receive ye the Holy Ghost," and He had come in to dwell in their bodies (John 20:22). The indwelling of the Spirit began when Christ was exalted in a resurrection body, as He promised in John 7:37–39. Yes, the apostles had everything—salvation, a call, training, instructions, the indwelling Spirit and joy—*everything but soul-winning power!* So Jesus commanded them, "Behold, I send the promise of my Father upon you: but tarry ye in the city of Jerusalem, until ye be endued with power from on high" (Luke 24:49).

What they needed was *power from on high!* Beloved brethren, we too need the supernatural, miracle-working power of God upon our ministry.

I am not talking here of a jabber in tongues nor of an ecstasy of feeling nor of sinless perfection. I do not mean that we are to seek a self-centered "experience" so that we may go about boasting that we are holier than others; and I do not care whether you call it *a baptism, a filling, an anointing, a pouring out of the Spirit,* or *a gift.* But God help us to see that we need the power of God, power to witness, so that souls will be saved, churches revived, and God become real and His presence blessed to thousands. "Ye shall receive power, after that the Holy Ghost is come upon you: and ye shall be witnesses unto me both in Jerusalem, and in all Judaea, and in Samaria, and unto the uttermost part of the earth" is what Jesus promised in Acts 1:8.

O preacher-brethren, we need power, power with God and power with men! Any theology, however orthodox, that leaves out the need for a holy enduement of the Spirit's power as manifested in the soul winning of the New Testament, is a barren desert with rainless clouds, a dry waterhole and a broken cistern! It is wicked presumption, modernism of the heart, infidelity in practice!

Whatever of self-judgment, of confession, of restitution, and self-crucifixion; whatever waiting on God, whatever surrender, whatever faith it takes, the one essential that the soul-winning man or woman must have is the power of the Spirit of God to attract, convict, enlighten and save sinners!

If it is to be greatly blessed of God and work soul-saving miracles, evangelistic preaching must boldly attack sin, must have holy earnestness and fervor, must depend upon the Word of God, must aim for definite results, and must have a definite enduement of the Holy Spirit.

Brethren, let us do God's kind of preaching and win souls. *"Do the work of an evangelist"!*

The Soul Winner's Feet

"And your feet shod with the preparation of the gospel of peace."—Eph. 6:15.

Soul winning begins with the feet! To our proud, haughty, human minds it would seem proper that soul winning would demand the most brilliant minds, the greatest education, the strongest possible backing of wealth and influence. But not so! Instead, soul winning is made a prosaic matter of the feet! That is the way of God. He has chosen by the foolishness of preaching to save men, instead of by the wisdom of angels or even the wisdom of this world. He has chosen the weak to confound the mighty. So soul winning is very largely a matter of consecrated feet.

A little reflection will show that the same principle is taught many times throughout the Bible. In the Great Commission the first two words are, "Go ye." Going is before teaching, preaching or baptizing! In Psalm 126:6, where God gives a wonderful outline of soul winning, we are told, "He that goeth forth and weepeth, bearing precious seed, shall doubtless come again with rejoicing, bringing his sheaves with him." Again, going is before sowing or reaping, or weeping or rejoicing.

God certainly demands that we put feet in soul winning. And when He wanted to make soul winners out of some fishermen, He said, "Follow me, and I will make you fishers of men."

Following comes before fishing, just as going comes before sowing. Walking comes before talking in God's plan.

In Luke 14 the work of a soul winner is clearly pictured. A man made a great supper and bade many. Now notice the activities of the servant (the model soul winner), and his lord's commands to him. "And he sent his servant at suppertime to say." You see, "going" comes before "saying." Again, "So that servant came, and shewed his lord these things." Soul winning is not all glory. A lot of it is coming back for further orders, when our message does not bring results.

Notice again: "Then the master of the house being angry said to his servant, Go out quickly into the streets and lanes of the city, and bring in hither the poor, and the maimed, and the halt, and the blind." "Go out" must be before "bring in." The feet have much to do with soul winning.

Then we find that the servant, after going out into the streets and lanes of the city, came back and reported that there was yet room. Notice the command, "And the lord said unto the servant, *GO* out into the highways and hedges, and compel them to come in, that my house may be filled." The same servant who had gone from house to house for the guests first invited and who then searched all the streets and lanes of the city for the poor, the maimed, the halt, and the blind, at last set out for the highways in the country and up and down the hedges to compel the people to come in! And between times he returned again and again to report to his boss.

That servant's main business was not inviting but going. Going took more time than anything else. Getting out the Gospel is largely a matter of footwork. And remember that one command was "go out quickly." I am sure that that servant was valued by his master, not for his eloquent speech nor for his tender pleading, but for faithful going!

And so all Christians are commanded to have "your feet shod with the preparation of the gospel of peace"!

Beautiful Feet

The feet of a soul winner are beautiful in God's sight. The Spirit of God tells us in Isaiah 52:7:

"How beautiful upon the mountains are the feet of him that bringeth good tidings, that publisheth peace; that bringeth good tidings of good, that publisheth salvation; that saith unto Zion, Thy God reigneth!"

Again, Nahum 1:15 is a similar passage, praising the feet of those who carry the Gospel message.

"Behold upon the mountains the feet of him that bringeth good tidings, that publisheth peace!"

In Romans 10:15 we have the same message:

"And how shall they preach, except they be sent? as it is written, How beautiful are the feet of them that preach the gospel of peace, and bring glad tidings of good things!"

How can one preach except he first goes? Of what use

is a mouth with a sweet message, unless the feet carry it? How beautiful are the feet of the soul winner!

I can well understand how the dear Saviour Himself washed the feet of the disciples. He meant it as a lesson in humility, yet someway He made the feet of a preacher grand and beautiful. The feet of the apostles trudged over the then-known world, carrying the Gospel.

Every preacher, every missionary, every soul winner ought to read carefully the story of Paul's missionary journeys with this in mind that Paul spent more time walking than he did preaching, and his feet got more exercise than his mouth! Paul not only preached publicly but also "from house to house" (Acts 20:20).

I was profoundly impressed one day in reading Acts 20:13, 14:

> *"And we went before to ship, and sailed unto Assos, there intending to take in Paul: for so had he appointed, minding himself to go afoot. And when he met with us at Assos, we took him in, and came to Mitylene."*

Paul was minded to go "afoot" from Troas to Assos, a distance, I suppose, of eighteen or twenty miles. I think it likely that on the crowded ship he would have no quiet place in which to meditate and pray, no time to seek the will and power of God. So he provided that his lesser companions should have the comfort of the ship while he walked.

And to make it more interesting yet, remember that in the same chapter the preceding verses tell how the night before he had preached until midnight, then brought back to life the young man who fell out of the third-story window, ate a midnight lunch and talked on till daylight!

Following that, then, Paul felt the need to walk a day-long journey to the next preaching place!

Beautiful feet of Paul! They were soul winner's feet. No wonder Paul could say of himself, "In labours more abundant." We often miss the point, so clearly taught in the Bible, that there is a severe price in toil to be a soul winner.

I can easily get a preacher willing to fill a pulpit and preach a sermon, but it is a difficult thing to get somebody to do house-to-house visitation—harder still to get Christians to take tracts and walk block after block giving out the message of life or spreading revival circulars and handbills. Christians do not realize that walking is the first part of soul winning.

Pearls are found in oysters in the bottom of the sea; diamonds are found in the dirt far below the surface of the ground in Africa; and the soul winner's joy is found in the midst of drudgery and toil. Precious souls are not won without going after them. It takes consecrated feet to be a soul winner!

Oh, may you who read this, develop feet that are beautiful in the sight of God, feet over which new converts in Glory will rejoice and say, "How beautiful are the feet of them that preach the gospel of peace, and bring glad tidings of good things!"

Have your feet been shod with the preparation of the Gospel of peace?

May I urge everyone who longs to win souls to set yourself to pay a price. You envy the soul winner's joy and well you may, but it costs far more than you know! Do not think lightly of his work. Perhaps you see only the platform work, the public speech, not the enormous amount of drudgery and going, the footwork that is necessary for anybody to be a soul winner for Christ.

"Shod With the Preparation—"

There are too many barefooted Christians. There are too many would-be soul winners who are not shod with the preparation of the Gospel of peace. Once "Uncle William" Mullins said about a certain problem that he faced, "Now this is going to be a battle of wits!" His wife, Mamie, replied, "That is just like you, William, entering into a battle half-armed." There are too many half-armed Christians entering into the battle with the Devil. The lesson here is that, if you want to win souls, then get ready.

I well remember that the first garments my dear father put on each morning were his socks. He didn't want his feet to get cold. And so a Christian every day is to prepare his mind and heart for soul winning. Put the shoes of the Gospel on your feet before you start out for the day!

First, I think this means that you need a new dedication to soul winning every day. The little song we sang in Sunday school a long time ago is good for every Christian:

> **I washed my hands this morning**
> **So very clean and white,**
> **And held them up to Jesus,**
> **To work for Him till night.**
>
> **Little feet be careful**
> **Where you take me to;**
> **Anything for Jesus,**
> **Only let me do.**

Your body is the temple of the Holy Spirit, which you have of God, and you are commanded to glorify God in your body. Then let God have your feet! Dedicate them to Him each day to carry the Gospel. A fire hose with a high pressure nozzle may shoot a stream of water hundreds of feet high, and that may do for putting out fires; but it will not do for carrying water to the sick and dying. That you must carry by hand, and perhaps hold the cup while they sip. My dear friend, you cannot shoot the Gospel to China from the home base; somebody must carry it there.

It is well enough to enclose tracts in letters. Every way to get out the Gospel is good, but some people will never be reached without the clasp of a warm hand or the earnest, searching gaze and the quiet word or sometimes the tear of one whose trudging feet have carried the Gospel in person.

Strangely enough, the Gospel goes better by retail than by wholesale. I believe in mass evangelism, but do not misunderstand mass evangelism. The great revivals are made up principally on the human side of thousands of details, steps taken, planning, inviting, advertising, sweating, crying and praying; and then the public preaching and singing often get all the credit!

So if you want to win souls, put your shoes on your feet every day. That means to store your mind and heart with Bible verses that you can take to those whom you seek to win. That means to plan your work. Depend upon the Holy Spirit to direct where you should go, whom you should see, and what you should say. Watch for the "breaks" in the game. Many a football game has been decided because an alert player blocked a punt or fell on the ball or snatched a pass not intended for him.

I have known some preachers who were unprepared when called upon to preach. I have always thought it shocking that any preacher should not have bait on his hook and his gun loaded all the time. The Christian's mind should be so set on soul winning, and his heart so prepared for soul winning, and his will so surrendered to the Spirit's leadership, that he can win souls at every opportunity.

Will you permit a bit of personal testimony? Some time ago I was called to a funeral of an old man whom I did not know, yet one who had plainly told his loved ones he was ready to meet Christ, his Saviour. I had never seen the man who died; I did not know any of his relatives or friends at the funeral. I did not know a single pallbearer, except one that I took with me; yet my heart was greatly moved, and I felt led to preach on John 3:16. I thought that surely these dear troubled souls, most of whom were unsaved, would be comforted by the thought that God so loved them as to give His Son.

At that funeral I preached a gospel sermon, almost as I would preach it in a revival campaign. I asked those who needed Christ to hold up their hands for prayer. Most of those present did. I asked those who would take Christ as Saviour to claim Him openly. A number did. When I returned from the cemetery (where I had the joy of winning two others), I thought back to the early morning when in my private devotions I had asked the Lord to help me win somebody that day. I tried to set my heart on soul winning. Through His mercy and help, I had in a small measure shod my feet with the preparation of the Gospel of peace.

Again, very humbly, permit me to give another illustration. One Saturday night I was called out of bed at 11:30 to marry a couple. I had risen at 5:30 in the morning; and at 6:00 I had gone to work on the open-air lot, preparing for the revival, digging holes for the light poles, cutting weeds, moving benches, setting light poles, and helping to build the giant screen for gospel pictures. It had been a busy, heavy day, and yet somehow my heart was moved to hunger over sinners and to pray for them. I had retired rather sadly because I had not won a soul that day.

When I went to the door and found that a dear friend had brought his sister and her sweetheart so I could perform the ceremony, I prayed while I dressed that God would give me wisdom. The young couple loved each other very dearly. It showed in their faces and in every act.

After the marriage ceremony, during which both were awed and moved by the Scriptures read and the sanctity of the step they were taking, I urged upon them the need to take Christ as Saviour both into their home and into their hearts. The young man first and then the girl claimed to trust in Christ.

After a time of counsel and as they were about to leave me at the door, the young man said, "Brother Rice, I am sorry to keep you up so late, but you have made me so very happy, and I believe that you are happy in our happiness!"

I do not win as many as I should, and I do not know how many opportunities I missed on that Saturday; but I do know that God helped me in the eleventh hour, at the time when these young hearts were tender, because early in the day I had committed myself to winning of souls and had shod my feet with the preparation of the Gospel of peace!

How many we could win if we were ready! Jesus won the woman at the well of Samaria because "he must needs go through Samaria." He had prepared and planned ahead of time to win that dear soul and others. He won her because His mind was not on food, as were the minds of His disciples, but on needy souls. He could say, "I have meat to eat that ye know not of" because He had shod His feet with the preparation of the Gospel of peace.

O my dear Christian, take time to get ready every day for soul winning! Study your Bible, ask God to cleanse your heart, seek divine wisdom in your plans. Secure the right tracts to give out, ask the Holy Spirit to give you the right words to say.

Philip the evangelist walked all the way from Samaria down to the road that leads from Jerusalem to Gaza which is desert (Acts 8). It must have been a long, tiresome journey, particularly for a great evangelist who was called away from the thrill of a marvelous revival. But Philip went. He had beautiful feet in God's sight! I am sure they seemed so to the eunuch, also. And the compassionate heart of God was so moved in love toward Philip that on the return journey He caught him away, and he was carried back by the Spirit to Azotus. He had been faithful in walking, so he got a ride, carried by the Holy Spirit! But the long walk of Philip would have been wasted if he could not have begun at Isaiah 53, the same Scripture that the eunuch was reading, and preached unto him Jesus!

Philip walked, but before he went walking that day he put on his shoes. He had his feet shod with the preparation of the Gospel of peace. He knew his Bible, he was led by the Spirit, and he had his heart prepared in sincere love for sinners.

A preacher can well afford to read his Bible. Elisha could well afford for a time to be simply the servant "which poured water on the hands of Elijah" (II Kings 3:11). Timothy could well afford to wash Paul's feet and write his letters, before he got to be the bishop of the great church at Ephesus. Any would-be soul winner can well afford to study his Bible, wait before God in prayer, and be filled with the Holy Spirit. Put on your shoes, brother, put on your shoes!

"The Gospel of Peace"

The soul winner's feet are to be shod with the preparation of the Gospel of peace. The good news is so sweet that the soul winner must enjoy it himself. The messenger of a king may carry a package or a letter whose seal he dare not break, but it is not so with God's messengers. The soul winner must know the Gospel that he is to take to the sinner. He must be able to say, "I have tried it myself." If you seek sinners, you must be saved yourself, and the sweet Gospel that won you must be fresh in your heart.

When Samson found the honey in the carcass of the lion he very properly carried some to his mother and father. But he carried it in his own hands, eating as he went! My dear brother, there is honey enough for all. Eat it and be filled with the Gospel of peace as you carry it to others.

Here is a strange thing, my brother! No verse of Scripture will ever be so sweet to you as that one which you have used in pointing some other soul to Christ. A preacher never understands other parts of the Bible as well as that portion of the bread of life which God has led him to break for others. The sweetest verses in my Bible are those used when I have preached with tears and power, and when others have been blessed.

It is a Gospel of peace that you carry, and part of the soul winner's preparation is the sweet enjoyment of the assurance of his own salvation. One who rejoices that his name is written in Heaven may get other names written there, too.

This Is Part of the Christian's Armor

And now comes a surprising lesson. The soul winner's shoes are part of his armor, part of his defense against Satan. In this same passage, Ephesians 6, we read in verses 10–15:

> *"Finally, my brethren, be strong in the Lord, and in the power of his might. Put on the whole armour of God, that ye may be able to stand against the wiles of the devil. For we wrestle not against flesh and blood, but against principalities, against powers, against the rulers of the darkness of this world, against spiritual wickedness in high places. Wherefore take unto you the whole armour of God, that ye may be able to withstand in the evil day, and having done all, to stand. Stand therefore, having your loins girt about with truth, and having on the breastplate of righteousness; And your feet shod with the preparation of the gospel of peace."*

Verse 15 tells how to be strong in the Lord and in the power of His might, as commanded in verse 10. It is part of the whole armor of God mentioned in verse 11, and these shoes are to be, put on "that ye may be able to stand against the wiles of the devil." Verse 12 tells us that we have a terrific battle on, not against flesh and blood, but against principalities, against powers, against the rulers of darkness, etc. Satan and all his evil spirits are around about the Christian. Therefore for his own safety, verse 15 tells us, the Christian must *have his "feet shod with the preparation of the gospel of peace"!*

In war and in football we are told that the "best defense is a good offense." The Christian who retires from the field of battle and lets souls go unhindered to Hell, is not safe from temptation; rather he is in greater danger. The Christian who really puts up a fight against Satan and snatches men as brands from the burning, will find that all about him God has put a wall of protection.

How many times I have been almost defeated, discouraged, downhearted, without a message to preach; but when I gave myself to personal soul winning and had the joy of seeing some saved, what joy, what close touch with God! How much easier it is to pray when you win souls! How much easier it is to resist temptation when your feet are shod with the preparation of the Gospel of peace!

The only safe place for a Christian is in the line of duty, and that is always in a path of soul winning. A young man called to preach said to me one day, "Brother Rice, if I do not preach I can't even live like a Christian." No doubt he was telling me the truth. One who follows the Spirit in soul winning can have the help of God in time of need. But if with a willful heart you pick your own path outside the will of God, you throw yourself open to a thousand evils and make yourself a prey to Satan and his evil spirits.

So, my brother, put the shoes of the Gospel on your feet and set out to win souls. Dedicate your feet to the blessed business of carrying Christ to sinners, and see that they are "shod with the preparation of the gospel of peace."

Unsaved Brothers!

"Then he said, I pray thee therefore, father, that thou wouldest send him to my father's house: for I have five brethren; that he may testify unto them, lest they also come into this place of torment."— Luke 16:27, 28.

One of the most moving passages in the Bible is Luke 16:19–31, where Jesus tells us of the rich man who died and was buried, "and in hell he lift up his eyes, being in torments." If we believe the Bible, we must take this account at face value. Jesus did not call it a parable. He gives the name of Lazarus, who lay at the rich man's gate full of sores. Lazarus was a real person, and the story is not fiction. The rich man was a real person. Doubtless, Jesus would have given his name, too, but for the loved ones or friends of the rich man who would be grieved or embarrassed. This account is a true story of what happened to two men, one who went to Heaven and the other who went to Hell.

Many say they do not like deathbed stories, but such men will have one of their own one of these days. It is foolish not to face the fact of death and the eternal certainties that are beyond death for the saved and the lost. Preachers should preach, as Jesus did, about a Paradise where the saved are comforted and consciously happy, and about a Hell where the unrepentant are "tormented in this flame," as the rich man said that he was.

Those who would be Christians must believe in a literal Hell of eternal, conscious torment for those who do not repent of their sins and seek salvation. No argument against a literal and eternal Hell of torment can weigh against the plain statement of the Lord Jesus Christ. Those who do not believe what Christ said should certainly not call themselves Christians nor pretend to believe the Bible. And those who would win souls must carry in the background of their minds this fundamental fact: men without Christ are lost, Hell-deserving and Hell-bound, and will lift up their eyes in Hell, tormented in flame, if they are not led to repent, to turn and trust Christ before they die unsaved.

What Do People Think About in Heaven?

We are all mightily interested in the unseen world. Our interest in those we love does not cease when they die. We know from the Bible that the soul does not cease to exist at death. There is life beyond death. Even savages instinctively know that this is true; and only the hardened, perverted, embittered and wicked cynic denies the eternal existence of the soul. The most natural thing in the world is to wonder what they are doing, these ones we have loved and lost awhile. Scores of times bereaved souls have come to me asking for light from the Word of God on what their loved ones are doing, whether they are happy, what they think, whether they know what is going on here on earth.

The saved in Heaven are deeply concerned about the race we run here on earth. The millions of angels who are our guardians and ministering spirits come and go constantly between earth and Heaven, as Jacob saw them in his dream. The rejoicing in the presence of the angels of God over one sinner that repents (Luke 15:7, 10) is shared by the saints of Glory. Heaven is concerned about soul winning. The love with which "God so loved the world" is shared by every redeemed soul in Heaven. The concern of Christ, the tender compassion of Him who poured out His soul unto death, the great love of the Saviour who is the Advocate and High Priest of every believer, are shared by the saved who are spiritually in the likeness of Christ. We know, then, that soul winning must be the chief concern of people in Heaven.

What People Think About in Hell

In Hell, too, people see things as they are; they face eternal verities. And that being true, people in Hell are concerned about soul winning.

The rich man in Hell died as he had lived, an unrepentant sinner. He did not love God when he lived, and he did not love God after he died. People do not repent in Hell. People are not good in Hell. As the tree when cut falls in the direction it leans, so men in Hell are still the same kind of men that they were when they lived. God's mercy is withdrawn, and good influences are absent; but the wicked, rebellious, sin-loving, Christ-rejecting soul of the sinner is still the same.

When he lived the rich man loved his five brothers. When he died he still loved his five brothers. He evidently led them in sin while he lived. Now that he is in Hell, he does not want them to "come into this place of torment."

He knows that unless they repent they ought to come and must come to the same torment and doom which had unexpectedly fallen upon him. Men see clearer in Hell than they do on earth. When the rich man lived, he did not expect to go to Hell when he died; he did not see his own danger. But now that he is in Hell, he knows why he is there, and he is desperately afraid for his unsaved brothers who are not concerned about themselves!

The rich man in Hell had two concerns. First, he was concerned to know if there was some way to alleviate the awful torment brought on by his sin. Second, even his own torment could not drown the cries of his scourging conscience. He felt accountable for his brothers and begged that they might be saved. We suppose that in Heaven there are two concerns: first, the unceasing joy and glory of a blessed salvation in the presence of Christ and the Father; and second, an interest in the salvation of men on this earth. So in Hell, we suppose there are two concerns: first, the awful realization and torments of the wages of sin; and second, a concern about those left behind on this earth. It becomes clear to the prayerful student of this account by Jesus, in Luke 16:19–31, that soul winning is a principal concern of those in Heaven and those in Hell!

Brothers! What a Tender Tie!

It is a part of the goodness and wisdom of God that children grow up in families. While beasts of the field are independent and self-sustaining in a few days or a few weeks after they are born, God planned that children should be under the nurture and care of parents for many years. Evolutionists are silly, illogical and blind when they say that marriage and the family are a product of evolution. No, marriage and the family are divine institutions! God gives time for the love and associations of father, mother, brothers and sisters to have their impact on character. God gives time for the ties between brother and sister, father and mother and the child to grow strong. Those tender ties ought never be severed. God meant the influence of brother on brother for good. We do not wonder that the rich man in Hell remembered his five brothers!

God intended that always in good or evil we should remember our brothers—those of our own family.

The ties of family are very intimate, very sweet, and very strong in lives that are truly Christian. The Bible teaches that children should honor their fathers and mothers and that they should requite or care for their aged parents. Among Jews, it was the command of God that a man marry his brother's wife and care for his brother's children. Proverbs 17:17 tells us that "a brother is born for adversity."

God allowed the brother under Jewish law to be the avenger of blood for his brother and slay the murderer if he could catch him before the guilty one reached the city of refuge (Num. 35:21).

What lessons there are for us in the brothers of the Bible! The best and the worst of a man comes out in relation to his brother.

Cain, the first man ever born, in a frenzy of hate and jealousy, killed his own brother. Then Cain lied to God and said, "Am I my brother's keeper?" Cain *was* his brother's keeper. Every man to whom God has given a brother is his brother's keeper. Even the rich man in Hell realized that!

A brother can love or hate his brother with a terrible intensity. Jacob and Esau were twin brothers. Esau was born first, but by trading and trickery Jacob got the father's blessing, though God had already chosen to give him the birthright, and it would have come so much more happily without his sin. What God had promised to give him, he seized by scheming. Hatred flared up in Esau's heart, and he swore to kill his brother as soon as their father Isaac died.

Jacob ran away to the land of Padan-aram to his mother's people and was there for twenty years without a sight of his loved ones. It is a touching and beautiful story in Genesis, chapters 32 and 33, which tell of his penitence, his eager efforts to please and win the favor of his brother Esau, his long night of prayer, wrestling with the angel of God, and then of how he and Esau met and hugged and kissed each other. Jacob said that he had seen his brother's face, "as though I had seen the face of God."

What sadness and bitterness when brother hates brother! What joy when they make reconciliation! What a tie is that of brotherhood, and how great is the influence of a brother! Who can read the story of Joseph and his brethren and not weep, as Joseph wept when he sent everyone else out of the room and said to the brothers who had sold him into slavery, "I am Joseph!" How he yearned over his baby brother Benjamin and laded his banquet plate with five times as much as the portion of the others! It is God that puts it into the heart of brother to love brother.

Memories of Youth, Childhood, Brothers

Abraham said gently but sternly to the rich man in Hell, *"Son, remember!"* People do remember in Hell! I am sure that the rich man wished he could forget, but memory is part of Hell's haunting torment. The rich man did remember, and I am sure that in Hell today he still remembers, *remembers,* REMEMBERS! And memory could not go back far down the line, calling to mind opportunities wasted, sins committed, light rejected, gospel messages scorned, without coming face to face with the fact of his five unsaved brothers. Doubtless it was true, and doubtless the rich man knew it, that the five unsaved brothers were impenitent and lost because they followed in his footsteps.

I suppose the rich man was an older brother. He died first. This rich man had had his own mansion, his own wealth, and the beggar "was laid at his gate." But the five brothers are back at their father's home, and from Hell the rich man cried for Lazarus to be sent to "my father's house; for I have five brethren." This man in Hell was the oldest of six brothers; now he faces the tormenting realization that he has led his five younger brothers in the ways of sin; that probably they, like himself, will die impenitent, condemned, and spend eternity in Hell.

In Hell one has plenty of time to remember, and the memories of childhood are strongest. Doubtless he remembered when each baby brother was born. He remembered their childish ways, their growing minds and bodies. These brothers had worked together, played together, and God knows that they had sinned together!

This writer has four brothers, one older and three younger than himself. We had a large family, and we five brothers had three sisters. I have thanked God many times for my brothers and sisters. The funniest things I ever knew to happen happened to us in the home on the farm. Many of the tenderest memories I have are of those early days with my brothers and sisters. My heart longs all the time for these who are mine by blood. We have the same childhood friends. We have the same ideals imbibed in the same home. We wept around the same graves. Our hearts are knit together by bonds that ought not be broken.

My two youngest brothers, Joe and Bill, were preachers. I think it possible, nay, probable, that had I not preached the Gospel, they would not have preached. An older brother has great influence. I well remember when I wrote my brother George, when I was in Baylor University, "Come on down to Baylor. You can room with me in this little attic room. I will help you through the best I can. And I have a girl picked out for you!" George came to Baylor, and we worked our way through together. I helped him all I could. A man is accountable for his brother. Incidentally, he married the girl!

When Joe planned to get married and didn't have the money, I raked up a few dollars for the necessary expense so that the boy might not delay his happiness. A brother is responsible for his brothers.

But with these memories are other memories which are sad. My brothers would have been better men had I been a better man. My influence has not been altogether and wholly good.

Brothers Should Win Brothers to Christ
The rich man in Hell remembered his brothers. He had lived his worldly, Christ-rejecting life before them. The five brothers had followed the sixth, who led them wrong. Throughout the ages of torment in Hell that rich

man will remember his sin against his brothers. If they went to Hell, as they may have done, can you imagine their meeting with the brother whose wickedness had led them to eternal torment? Perhaps a brother's love was turned to hate by the ruin which a brother's sin had brought. They sinned, and they deserved Hell, but perhaps they would have sought and accepted the free mercy of God but for the example of their brother.

Dear reader, if you have an unsaved brother, I beg you by everything that is holy, win him while you can.

People sometimes say, "Brother Rice, you know how it is. A man's own family won't pay any attention to him." Oh, yes, they will, if he means business. That thought is a deception of the Devil. Brother will listen to a brother more quickly than he will to an outsider. The ties of blood are stronger.

To be sure, we cannot influence our brothers if we live in hypocrisy. Lot could not influence his own sons-in-law, but neither could he influence anybody else. Any man who takes Christ as Saviour and lives a transformed life can have influence over his own brothers.

When Andrew was saved, "he first findeth his own brother Simon, and saith unto him, We have found the Messias, which is, being interpreted, the Christ. *And he brought him to Jesus*" (John 1:41, 42). Old stubborn-hearted, loud-mouthed, blustering Simon Peter must have been a pretty hard man to influence. He wanted to lead, not to be led. This old cursing fisherman had his own opinions and was quick to express them. I have an idea that he was older than Andrew, though the Bible does not say. Certainly he had the stronger character of the two. But when Andrew came, the first thing after he was saved, and said, "We have found the Messias," he brought Simon Peter to Jesus right away!

Oh, you can win your brothers in many cases, and I pray as I write these words that you will determine to do so.

One Sunday morning when I preached on this subject and asked how many in the audience had unsaved brothers, I suppose two-thirds of the congregation held their hands. If Christians who read this would win their own brothers at any cost, what a revival would sweep the land! What rejoicing, what hallelujahs, what happy homes, what glory to Christ!

"And Thy House"

God clearly intends that every human tie be used in soul winning. Mothers should use a mother's influence to win their children. So with the father. Sweethearts should win their lost sweethearts (though it is doubtful if Christians ought ever to have sweethearts who are unsaved. Certainly, the saved should never marry the unsaved). The teacher should win her pupil; the brother, his brother.

When the jailer came trembling and fell down before Paul and Silas and asked them, "What must I do to be saved?" the inspired answer of the apostles was, "Believe on the Lord Jesus Christ, and thou shalt be saved, *and thy house.*" The jailer was to believe, but the promise was not only for him; it was for his household! Even in the very act of salvation, the jailer was taught that he must win his family, he must tell them the same story and teach them to trust in Christ, as he himself had trusted Him. And the heart rejoices to read further on in the same chapter how that family, all saved and all baptized, gathered around the table past the midnight hour, after Paul and Silas had their wounds dressed, and ate their belated supper. The jailer and his family were happy, "believing in God with all his house."

There once came to my office in Dallas, Texas a man from Fort Worth who long had been a Christian. When he attended our Bible conference, he told how he had come to Dallas to see a lost brother and happily had led him to accept Christ. Now on this second trip, he told of the conversion of another brother. The second brother had been out in California, and the Fort Worth man, Mr. Conner, began to pray for his soul. He asked his Sunday school class to pray. On Monday night they had a special prayer meeting, praying that God would save Mr. Conner's brother. They prayed late and earnestly, and God seemed to hear. The next Wednesday morning, in California, the brother was strangely moved with a strong desire to see his loved ones back in Texas, so he got in his car and began the trip to Fort Worth. Now let Mr. Conner tell the story:

"I got him in my car, and we drove out on the Jacksboro highway. I asked him why he came back to Texas, and he told me he just suddenly became hungry to see his brothers. I told him how I had trusted the Lord, how our other brother had been saved, and how we had prayed for his soul. Then I took the Bible and showed him how to be saved, and there in my car he trusted Christ. We drove back into Fort Worth to tell the rest of the family." Mr. Conner's face beamed with joy as he told us the story of his brother's salvation.

Win your brother while you can. See him if possible. If not, write him. Begin to pray earnestly for his salvation.

Two other worlds are concerned about sinners. "There

is joy in the presence of the angels of God over one sinner that repenteth." Heaven longs to see the salvation of your brothers. Christ longs to save them. This is the thing nearest His heart. He came to seek and to save the lost.

In Hell men are lifting their cries, begging that someone be sent to warn their brothers who live here unsaved. If in the eternal worlds of bliss and torment the principal concern is the salvation of sinners, surely you should win your brothers while you can. Do not depend on others; do your part today to win your own brothers, and the brothers of others who are pleading for them in Hell.

Decide for Christ Today!

Dear reader, why not persuade some unsaved people to read these Scriptures, and urge upon them to confess their sins to God and trust Christ for forgiveness and salvation today!

"For God so loved the world, that he gave his only begotten Son, that whosoever believeth in him should not perish, but have everlasting life. For God sent not his Son into the world to condemn the world; but that the world through him might be saved. He that believeth on him is not condemned: but he that believeth not is condemned already, because he hath not believed in the name of the only begotten Son of God."—John 3:16–18.

My Decision for Christ

If you will here and now decide for Christ, taking Him as your own Saviour, will you not sign the following decision, then copy it in a letter and mail it to me? I will be so glad to rejoice with you over your salvation and will send you a letter of counsel and encouragement. Decide and sign it today and let us hear from you.

Dr. Shelton Smith
P. O. Box 1099
Murfreesboro, TN 37133

Dear Dr. Smith:

Realizing that I am a guilty, lost sinner, but believing that Christ died for my sins on the cross and rose again from the grave, I here and now accept Him as my personal Saviour, depending on Him to forgive all my sins, change my heart and give me everlasting life now, as He promised. I am glad to confess Him as my Saviour, and I sign my name to claim Him. I intend to live for Him, beginning today, and rely on Him for help.

Date_____

Name_____

Address_____

_____

If you have taken Christ as your own Saviour, then be sure to confess Him openly before men (Matt. 10;32); get in with the people of God, read your Bible daily, let the Lord Jesus be the Master of your whole life, and set out to be a soul winner for Him.

For a complete list of available books, write to:
Sword of the Lord Publishers
P. O. Box 1099
Murfreesboro, Tennessee 37133.

(800) 251-4100
(615) 893-6700
FAX (615) 848-6943
www.swordofthelord.com